IMAGES
of America

WORCESTER

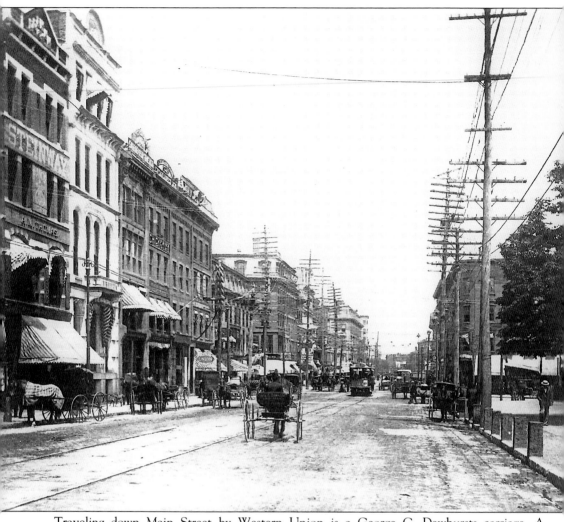

Traveling down Main Street by Western Union is a George C. Dewhursts carriage. A manufacturer and dealer in carriages and wagons of every description, Dewhursts Carriage Repository's motto was "Large sales at small profits."

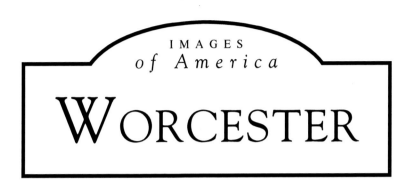

IMAGES
of America

WORCESTER

Compiled by
Lois R. Yeulenski

ARCADIA
PUBLISHING

Published by Arcadia Publishing
Charleston, South Carolina

Printed in the United States of America

For all general information contact Arcadia Publishing at:
Telephone 843-853-2070
Fax 843-853-0044
E-mail sales@arcadiapublishing.com
For customer service and orders:
Toll-Free 1-888-313-2665

Visit us on the Internet at www.arcadiapublishing.com

Dedicated to my son, Tom

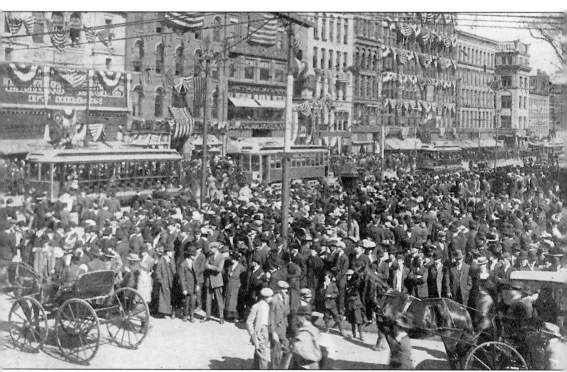

The crowds here are waiting patiently on Front Street for President Taft and his entourage to pass en route to the Train Service Men's Convention on April 3, 1910. President Taft had been visiting with his aunt Delia C. Torrey in Millbury before traveling to Worcester.

Contents

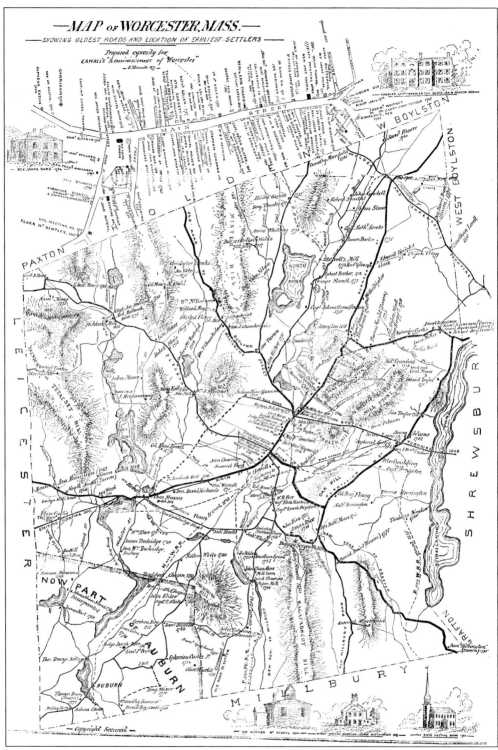

An 1877 map of Worcester from C.A. Wall's *Reminiscences of Worcester*.

Introduction

In 1674 Daniel Gookin smoked a peace pipe with the Native Americans then occupying the hill country some 50 miles west of Boston. Then, presenting them with 2 coats, 4 yeards of cloth and some money, the whole estimated at a worth of 12 pounds sterling, Gookin received a deed for 8 square miles of land called Quinsigamond. The new settlement was named Worcester after the market town in England.

For the next four decades Gookin's purchase was by and large uninhabitable by the English. So far removed from the coast and on a direct line between the Native American hunting frounds in the Berkshires and the Atlantic coast, the first two settlements attempted both failed, the victim of the ongoing struggle between the English and the Native Americans. However, in 1713, Jonas Rice led a group of colonists in beating back the attacks and establishing a citadel half a mile square. Until the French and Indian wars resulted in driving the Native Americans across the Hudson Rivers, the settlers returned to the citadel each night where they lived in individual huts.

For much of the eighteenth and nineteenth century Worcester continued a steady growth as a market town for the citizens who began to move west from the coast to find better farming land. During the American Revolution the area was a beehive of spy activity as both British and American operatives moved between Boston and the Berkshires.

With the coming of the Industrial Revolution the city of Worcester underwent major changes. Worcester was limited by the fact that it is not located on a major waterway, but a combination of citizen inventiveness and the siting of Worcester as a railroad hub created the right conditions for diverse industrial development.

Initially men such as Stephen Salisbury II and W.T. Merrifield built large factory buildings and leased them to small industries, thus allowing manufacturers to start up with minimal outlay of capitol. The effect was staggering. William Crompton's loom invention began a textile production boom. Osgood Bradley began the manufacture of railroad cars for the Boston and Worcester railroad in 1835. Dr R.L. Hawes produced the first successful machine for manufacturing envelopes, making Worcester the largest envelope manufacturer in the world at one point.

Westward expansion in the United States gave Worcester another industry, plain and barbed wire. From hoop skirts to pianos to the fencing of the American west, wire was a major commodity. Much of it was produced in Worcester. At various times in the nineteenth century, Worcester industries produced more looms, valentines, emery wheels, envelopes, corsets, carpets, leather goods, paper-box machinery, organ keys, musical reeds, paper-making.

Lois R. Yeulenski
November 1994

One

Downtown

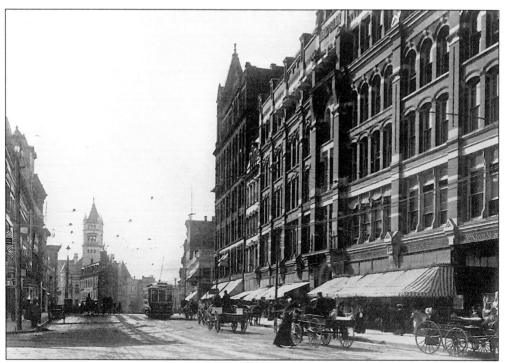

Across from Franklin on Main Street there was once a terrace—similar to the one on Court Hill—which extended as far as Chatham Street. This section was known as Nobility Hill, and it housed aristocrats until 1869, when it was demolished. The site was then occupied by the Boston Store until November 13, 1973, when the store finally closed its doors, ending a 102-year history in the city.

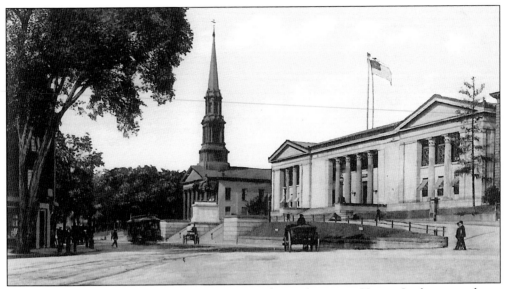

This view of Main Street from Lincoln Square shows the Court House. In front stands an equestrian statue of General Charles Devens, Worcester's most celebrated Civil War hero. The statue stands as a memorial to the men of Worcester County who died in the War for the Union.

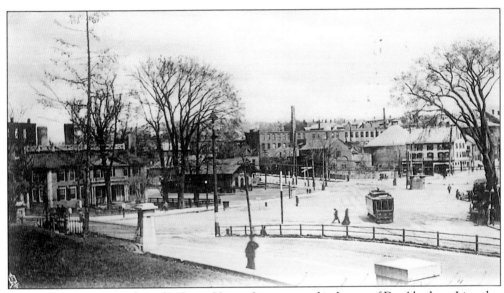

Lincoln Square, as seen from the Court House. It was named in honor of Dr. Abraham Lincoln, who kept an apothecary shop near where the Court House now stands. On the north side of the square can be seen the Salisbury Mansion, built in 1770. Formerly Lincoln Square was the center of fashion and wealth in Worcester, but now it is all business.

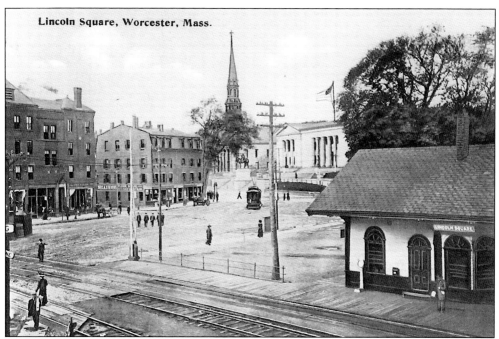

Lincoln Square, Worcester, Mass.

Lincoln Square Station can be seen in this view of Lincoln Square. President Grant arrived here in 1869 and was escorted to the Bay State Hotel, where he was served dinner.

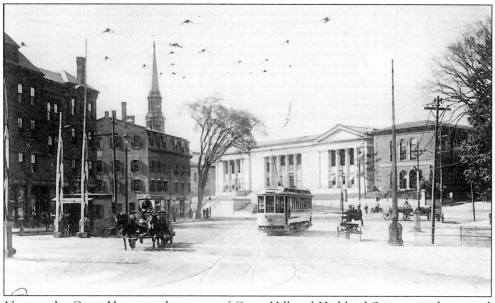

Next to the Court House, at the corner of Court Hill and Highland Street, was the second building of the American Antiquarian Society. This was where George Bancroft often came when writing his *History of the United States*. Across the street from the Court House, where the Marriott now stands, once stood the home of Timothy Bigelow, the renowned patriot.

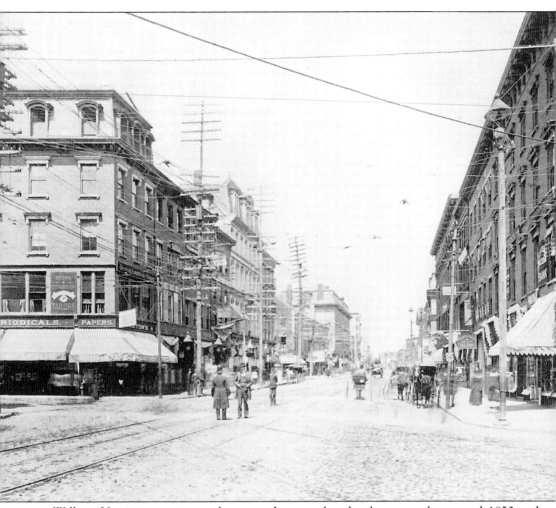

William Harrington, a tavern keeper and grocer, bought the corner lot around 1850 and erected the block known as Harrington Corner. Near the center of Harrington Corner was a huge elm tree which had a watering trough beneath it for horses. By the time this picture was taken, there was no longer water for horses, but there was Easton's for the human population: an ice cream parlor, newsstand, and cigar store, Easton's was a popular meeting place for over seventy years before it closed on July 30, 1964.

The Slater Building can be seen in this view of Main Street looking north. This land, from Pleasant Street to near Walnut Street, was originally part of the Curtis grant of land in 1675. The first pianos in Worcester were manufactured by Marsh and Emerson on this site.

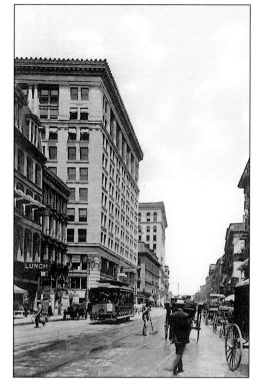

A view of Harrington Corner from City Hall in 1903. Electric trolleys may have replaced the horse-drawn cars, but horses were still pulling carriages and wagons. People were very proud of their family horses but were willing to share the road with the increasing number of more modern trolley cars.

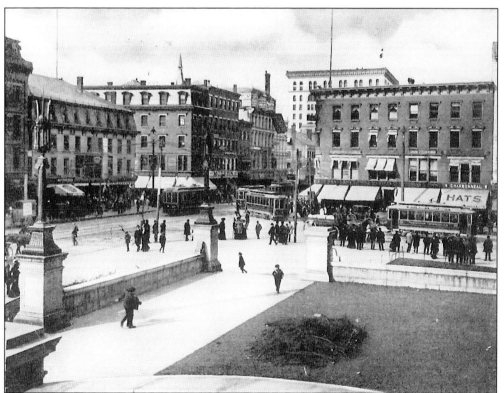

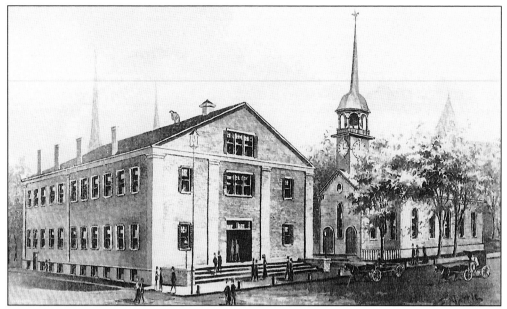

The Old Town Hall, built in 1824, stood on the corner of Main and Front Streets. It was two-and-a-half stories tall, with a basement which was used for stores along the Front Street side. It was used as a town hall until 1848, when it became City Hall. These walls have heard many great men, including President Adams (1826), Daniel Webster (1848), and Abraham Lincoln on September 12, 1848, when he addressed a Whig meeting. Next to the Old Town Hall stood the Old South Meeting House. It was from the western porch of this historic place of worship that the Declaration of Independence was first publicly read in New England, on July 14, 1776.

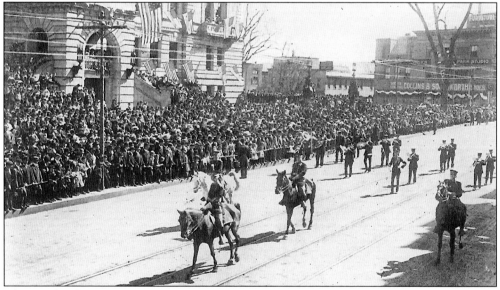

The people of Worcester loved parades and knew how to welcome public figures. This parade was one of the largest in Worcester's history. Passing City Hall on April 3, 1910, is the Train Service Men's Association on the way to a convention at Mechanics Hall, where President Taft addressed a full house.

14

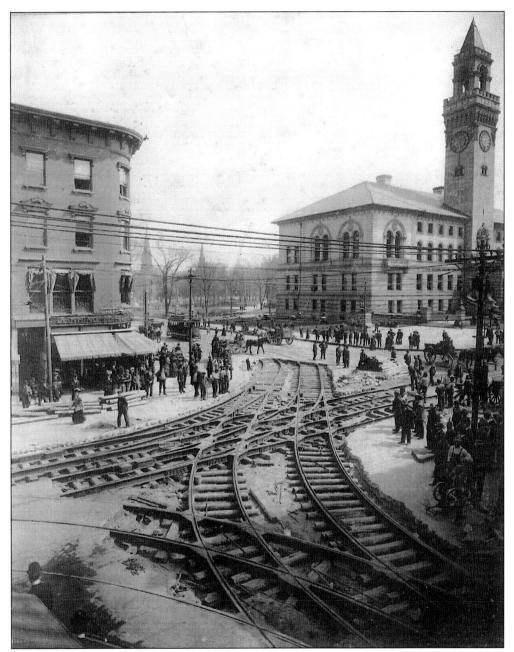

This view is of Harrington Corner from Pleasant Street, at the turn of the century. The street has been torn up around the trolley tracks, and judging from the wood rails and nails on the side of the street, it appears that the tracks are being repaired. It must have been very difficult for pedestrians crossing the street in order to shop at D.H. Eames Co., a clothing store.

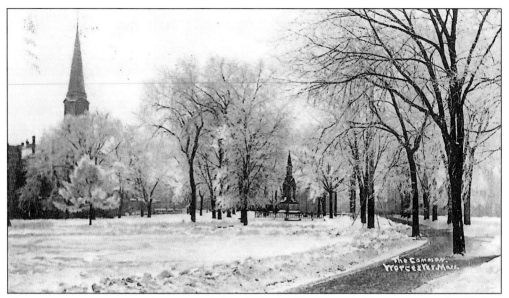

Here we see a snow-covered common behind City Hall, surrounded by trees coated with ice. Bigelow Monument in the background is a reminder that this was once the old training field during the days of the Revolutionary War.

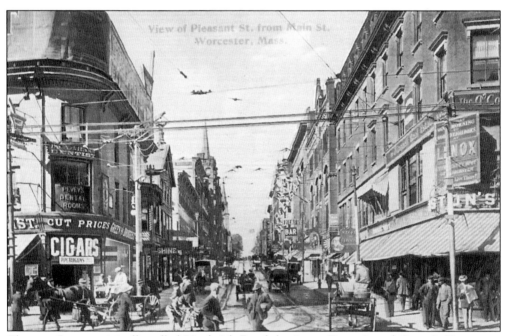

Pleasant Street, originally called Hardwick Road, begins at Easton's and Green's Drugstore. Notice, in front of Easton's, the gentleman leaning against the pole reading his newspaper.

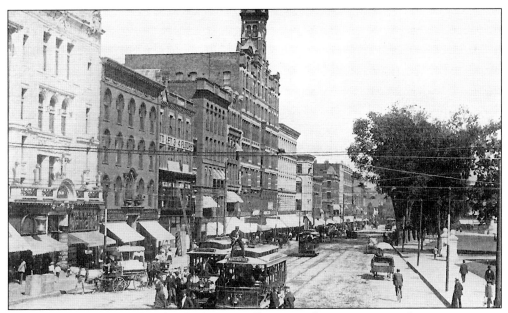

Front Street in 1903 was lined with electric trolley cars and wagons. at time there was a variety of transportation on a street that is now constantly busy with cars: note on the right a man in his wagon shaded by an umbrella and behind him a man pedalling his bicycle.

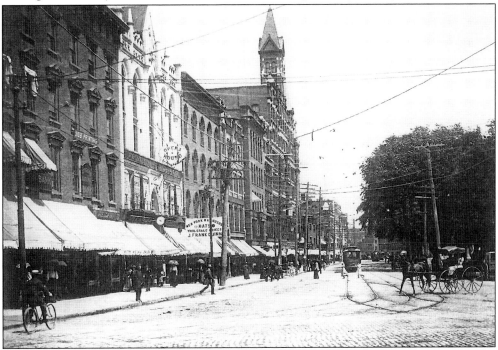

Front Street in 1894. Next to the Citizen's National Bank is the Front Street Opera House. In 1897 Jules E. Offner leased the building and changed the name to the Bijou Theatre. He showed "first class vaudeville at popular prices," installed the first moving picture machine, and continued in the theatrical business until February 18, 1898, when his building burned to the ground. He and his wife barely escaped from the fire with their lives.

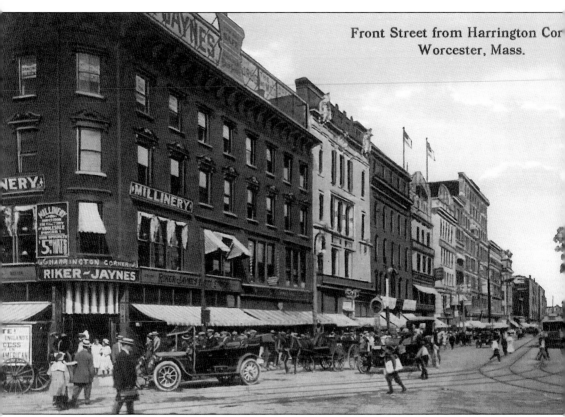

Front Street began to flourish around the turn of the century. Main and Front Streets were the center of the business district, and remained so for many, many years. Riker-Jaynes Drugstore, on this corner, is best remembered as Liggetts, with Diamond Jewelers on the second floor.

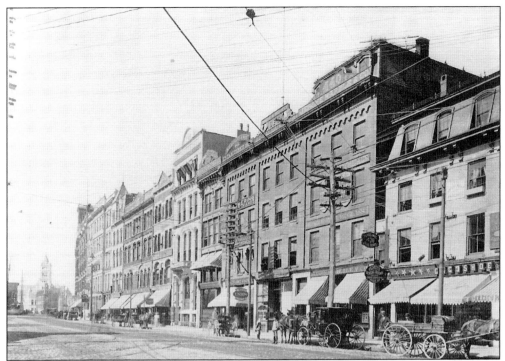

Pevey's Dental Rooms can be seen in this view looking south down Main Street in 1895. On the outside of the same building note the Employment Parlors advertisement. At 440 Main Street is the *Worcester Spy* building, with Western Union and Rebboli following it.

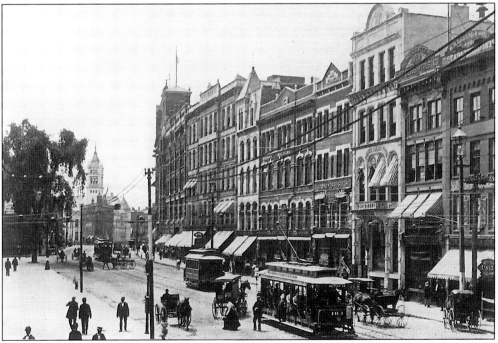

In 1903, riding down Main Street past the People's Savings Bank, is trolley #183 bound for Brittain Square. If you look closely, it seems as if a head-on collision is about to take place.

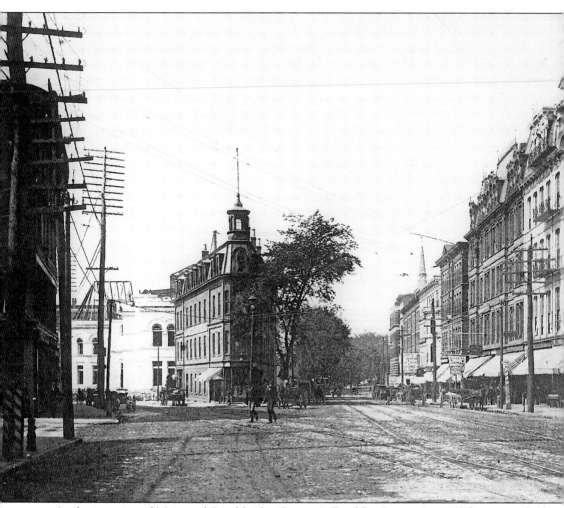

At the junction of Main and Southbridge Streets is Franklin Square. In 1893 horse cars had been abandoned and electric cars reintroduced. This progress unfortunately forced many shade trees on principal streets to give way to telephone poles and interlacing wires.

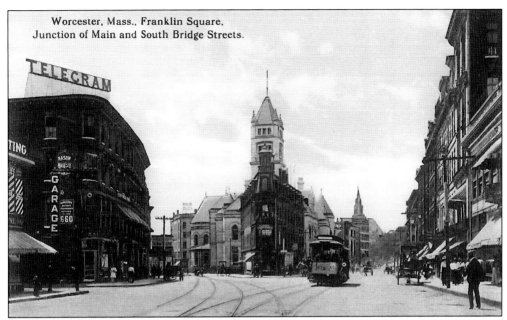

This flatiron building stood at Franklin Square in front of the old post office. Note the *Telegram* sign on top of the building which is now the Showcase Cinemas.

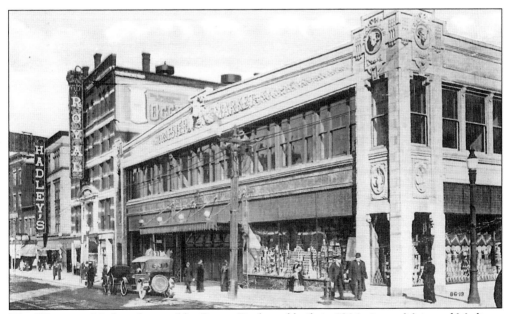

The Worcester Market, designed by Oreste Zirole and built in 1914, sits on Main and Madison Streets and at the time was the largest of its kind in the United States. The entire plant had an area of 90,000 square feet and a storage capacity of 1,500 tons.

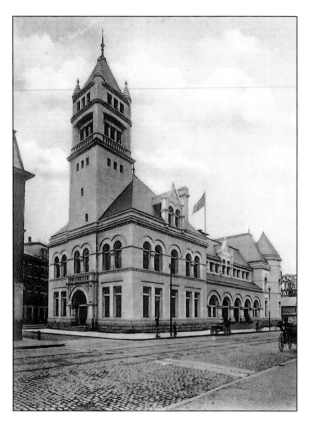

The Worcester Post Office, built in 1896 at Main and Southbridge Streets, was the first one owned by the government. It cost $568,365, nearly as much as City Hall, but was lacking in almost every area, including architectural design, capacity, arrangement, and lighting. It was massive and distinctively ugly. It was torn down in 1930.

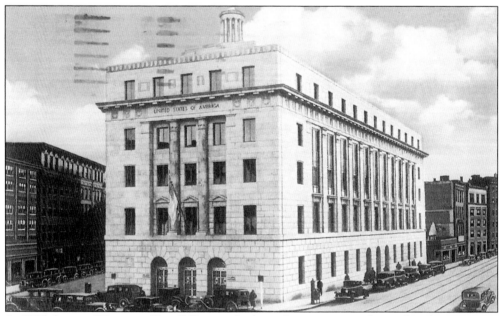

In 1932 the new Worcester Post Office was built on the same site and served as the main post office for many years.

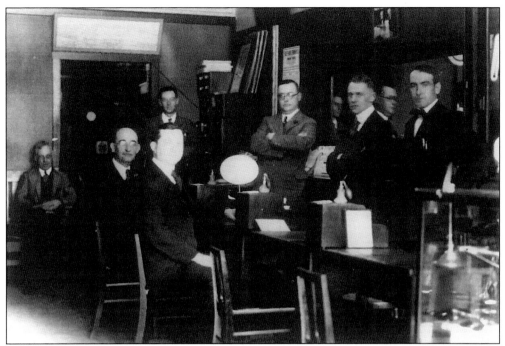

Magay and Barron Opticians, of 368 Main Street, was opened in 1912 by J.O. Magay. A third generation eye center operated by his son, R.A. Magay, is now located at 460 Lincoln Street and managed by his grandson, James G. Magay. Standing in front of the mirror are: (from left to right) J.O. Magay, proprietor; F. Patch; and R.T. Barron. (James Maguy)

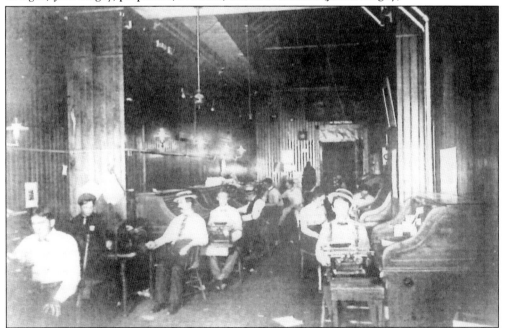

In 1901, the *Worcester Spy* was located at 282 Main Street. The reporters all had roll-top desks with typewriters at arms length. Notice that the men still have on their straw hats, even though they are inside.

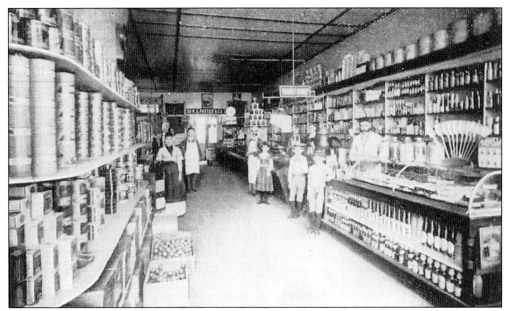

G.F. Conant & Co. (successors to W.O. Patten & Co.), located at 563 Main Street opposite the post office, were dealers in "Plain and Fancy Groceries," with the best butter, tea, and coffee in the city in 1895. Their motto was "We aim to sell not the cheapest goods, but the BEST for the prices charged." Notice the fan of flyswatters in the foreground.

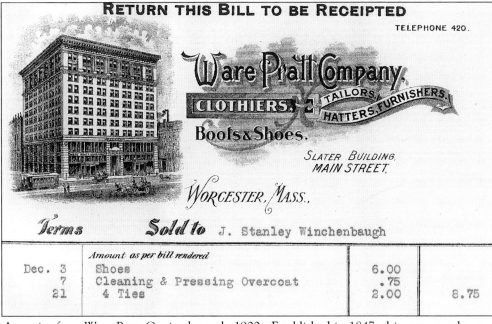

A receipt from Ware Pratt Co. in the early 1900s. Established in 1847, this store was known for the consistent quality and good style of the clothing it sold. Note the three-digit telephone number: at this time very few numbers were needed as the cost of a telephone was beyond the means of most people.

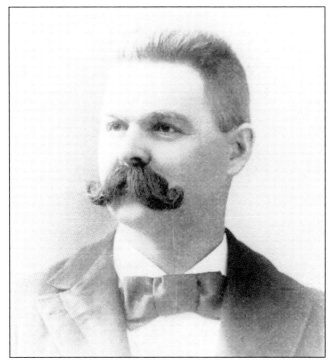

Dr. F.H. Kendrick practiced dentistry at 518 Main Street. In the 1880s the cost of removing a tooth was 25¢, and a new set of teeth could be bought for between $7 and $9.

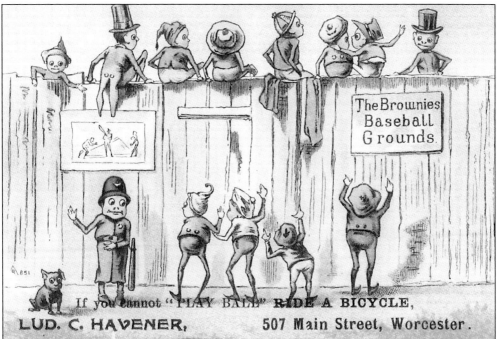

The Brownies Baseball Grounds

If you cannot "PLAY BALL" RIDE A BICYCLE,

LUD. C. HAVENER,   507 Main Street, Worcester.

In the 1890s Lud C. Havener had "the largest and greatest variety of bicycles in the city at a price to suit all." Bicycles were ridden by both men and women, and bicycle races were a very popular sport at the time. Worcester had its own champion, Marshall W. (Major) Taylor, known as the fastest bicycle rider in the world. In 1899 he put Worcester on the world map by winning the American championship.

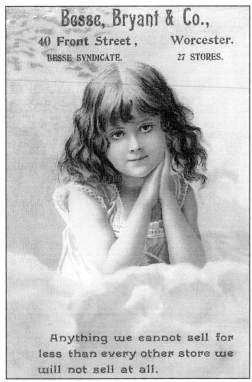

Besse, Bryant & Co.,

40 Front Street,   Worcester.

BESSE SYNDICATE.   27 STORES.

Anything we cannot sell for less than every other store we will not sell at all.

Besse, Bryant & Co. owned a store at 40 Front Street. This advertisement announces "Bargains in Fall Style Headwear." Creased soft fur hats—black or brown—were 50¢. All men's winter hats—normally 50¢— were on sale for only 38¢. Boston Derbys, Lamson & Hubbard, Dunlap, and Knox hats were all $1.45.

C. Rebboli & Son was founded in 1874 by Charles Rebboli. Born in Italy in 1837, he came to America in 1864 and to Worcester in 1871, where he started his confections, catering, bakery, and restaurant business. The restaurant was located in the rear of the store, and their phone number and address on Main Street were the same: "444."

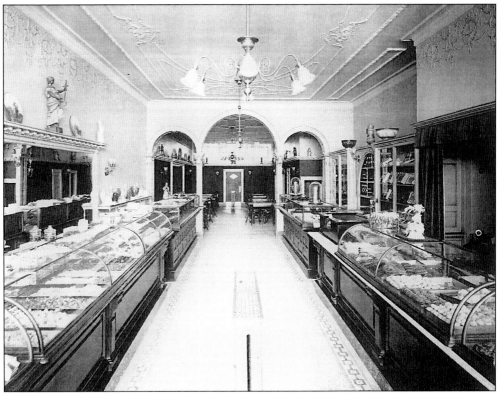

Two

People

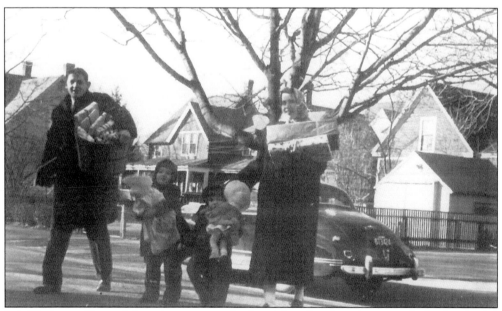

It is Christmas Day and there is no snow to be found, but that doesn't seem to be bothering the Randalls. Barbara and Jackie Randall look very content holding their dolls from Santa Claus, while their mother, Mary, smiles proudly at the camera. (Scott Randall)

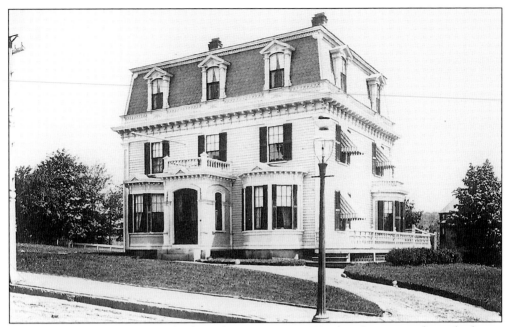

This house, built in 1855 by Charles Whittemore at 10 Windsor Street, was later the home of Colonel Fred W. Wellington. In 1870 it was remodeled in the French Second Empire style: brackets were added to the corners and a mansard roof was finished with pedimented dormers and twisted rope moldings on the corners. The Wellington Rifles, Worcester's 3rd Company in the 2nd Regiment, was named after Colonel Wellington as a tribute to his long and distinguished service in the militia.

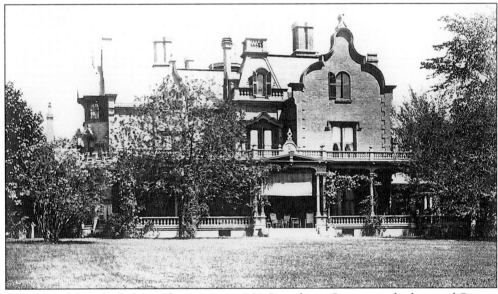

This beautiful brick Gothic-style mansion at 121 Providence Street was the home of George Crompton, the inventor and sole owner of the Crompton Loom Works. In 1886, at the time of his death, he was the largest employer in Worcester and possessed one of the city's grandest estates.

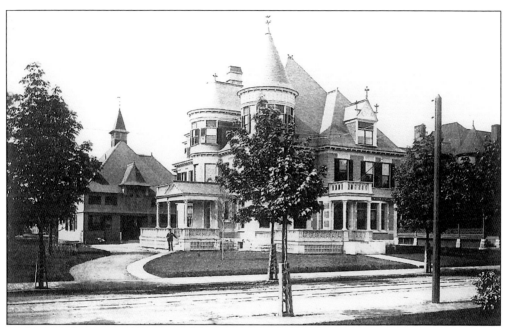

William H. Burns was the owner of this Victorian-style house at 31 Sever Street. Mr. Burns, a manufacturer of women's underwear, was born in Charlestown in 1856 and came to Worcester in 1883. It is not known if the man standing by the side porch is indeed Mr. Burns.

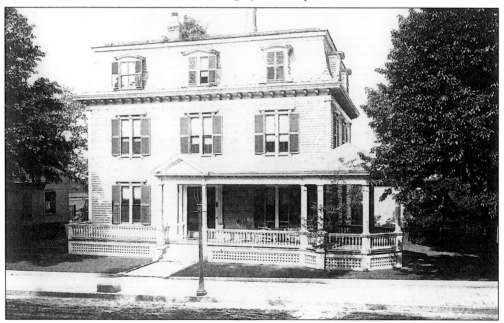

Samuel Heywood, a manufacturer of boots and shoes, lived in this house at 41 Oak Avenue, which is another example of French Second Empire-style architecture. When Worcester was known throughout the country for its manufacturing, there was great demand for Heywood products not only in the United States but also in Canada, England, Honolulu, Havana, and other foreign markets. His employees recognized Mr. Heywood as an appreciative personal friend, as well as a just and kind employer.

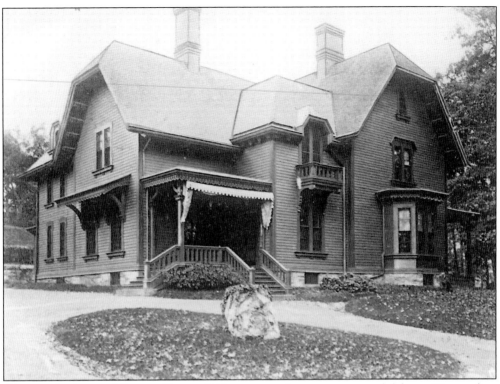

This was the home of Senator George Frisbee, a great lawyer, orator, and debater. He was first elected senator in 1877 and served in that capacity until his death in 1904. A statue of Frisbee stands on the northwest corner of City Hall.

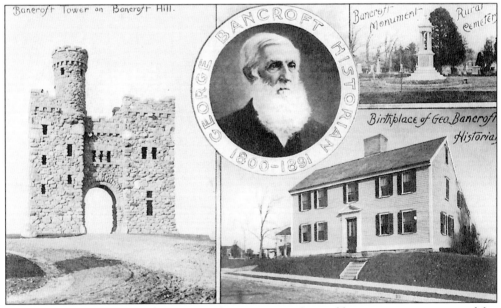

George Bancroft was a great historian and statesman, and served his country as secretary of the navy. His most lasting legacy is the US Naval Academy at Annapolis, which he founded.

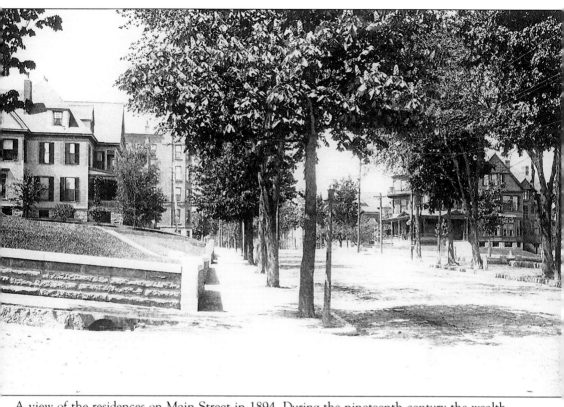

A view of the residences on Main Street in 1894. During the nineteenth century the wealth created by industry and business in Worcester was reflected in the homes of its prominent men and women.

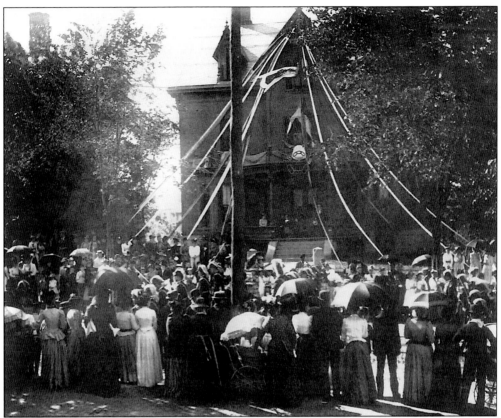

The Odd Fellows' procession passing the home of T.H. Dodge at 766 Main Street, after the dedication of the Odd Fellows' Home on June 22, 1892.

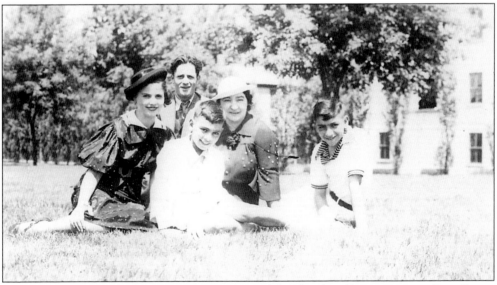

This 1938 photograph shows Mary Ruggieri and her brother Dominic, as well as Bessie Servideo with her sons Frank and Angelo, all sitting on the grass at Notre Dame Cemetery in their fashionable clothes.

Thomas H. Dodge was a distinguished lawyer, inventor, and public benefactor. His generous contributions aided greatly in building the Trinity Methodist Church, and he later helped to build the new Union Church and the Piedmont Church. He also assisted the Worcester Natural History Society in establishing summer schools for the young, but he is probably best remembered for donating the land that would eventually become the site of the Odd Fellows' Home and Dodge Park. In addition, Dodge enacted reform in the postal system, and his recommendation that "Dead Letters: be returned to the writer rather than staying at the post office" has been turned into law.

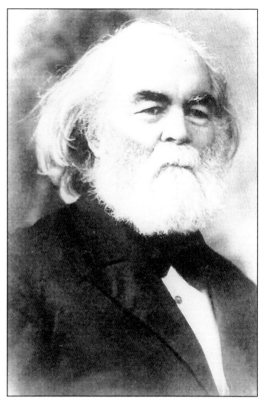

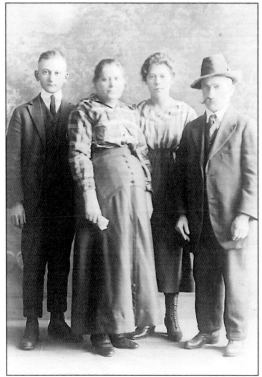

A Dellasanta family portrait showing Antonia and Tomaso with two of their four children, Amato and Regina.

33

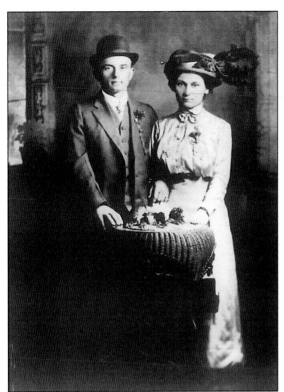

The wedding portrait of Henry Verdini and Antonia Dellasanta taken on April 30, 1913. Mrs. Verdini had purchased her dress at Denholm's, the Boston Store on Main Street. Mr. Verdini was the founder of the Verdini Milk business. (Donna Murphy)

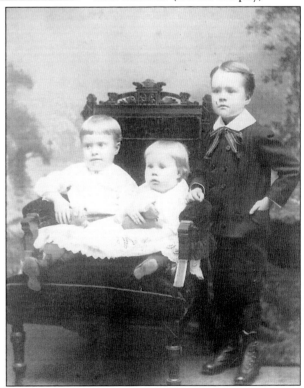

A Victorian-style portrait of the Houghton children. Arthur Houghton stands proudly next to his sisters Mabel and Cecile. Note Arthur's high laced boots. (Scott Randall)

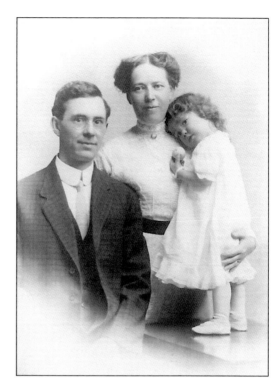

A portrait of the Joynes family. John H. and Florence Kelley pose with their adorable daughter Marion. (Marilyn Orr)

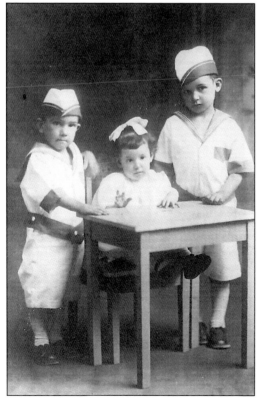

Eva Verdini posing with her brothers Carroll (left) and Arthur (right) in 1919. Their parents (see opposite page) obviously took great pride in their children. The sailor suits are breathtaking.

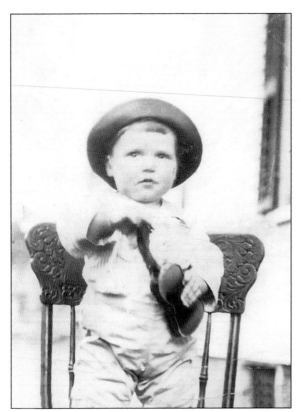

Looks like we have a musician in the family: Arthur Verdini stands on a pressed-back chair tuning up his stringed instrument in 1916. I bet those cheeks have been pinched more than once!

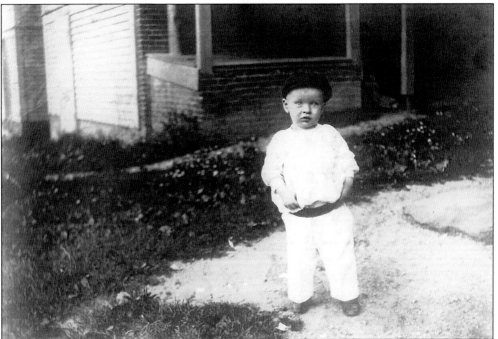

Arthur Johnson standing on Hollywood Street on the early 1900s. Wouldn't he be perfect for "Spanky and Our Gang"? (Nancy Johnson)

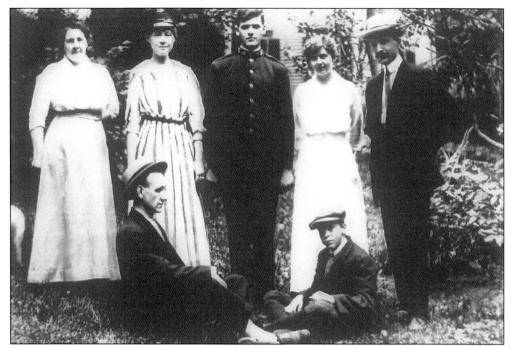

"Thursday Afternoon Coffee." Every Thursday afternoon, on their day off, these Swedish women and their boyfriends would meet at Amanda Johnson's house for coffee. (Nancy Johnson)

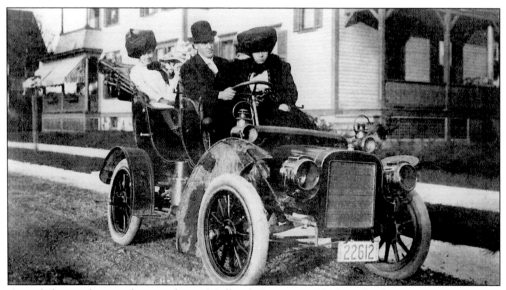

A stylish gentleman driving down Midland Street in 1910 with three women sporting fashionable hats. (Scott Randall)

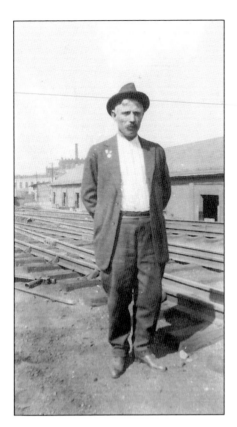

Michael Ruggieri in 1915, standing by the railroad tracks of the Boston & Albany Railroad Company where he was employed.

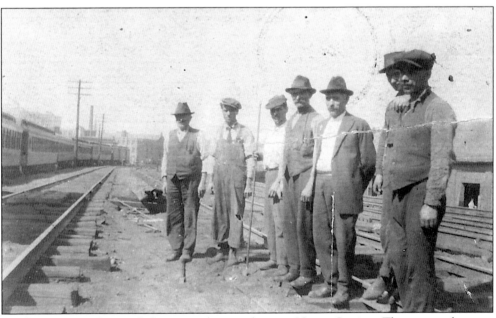

Mr. Ruggieri standing with his co-workers at the new Union Station. These were the men responsible for the train tracks. They laid many hundreds of tracks between them.

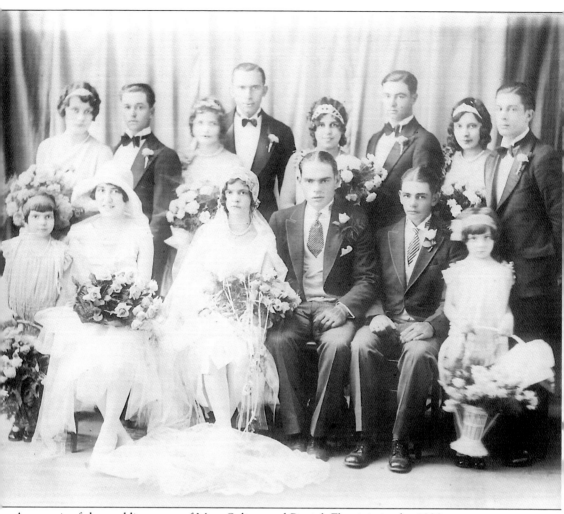

A portrait of the wedding party of Mary Solitro and Patrick Flaminio in the 1920s.

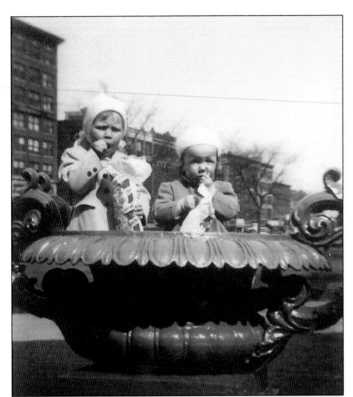

Two unidentified children enjoying their popcorn in what appears to be either a planter or fountain on the common. (Harriet Alukas)

Barbara and Jacqueline Randall and a friend on 16 Winslow Street. It must have been cold out that day—the three of them are in their snowsuits and rubber boots. (Scott Randall)

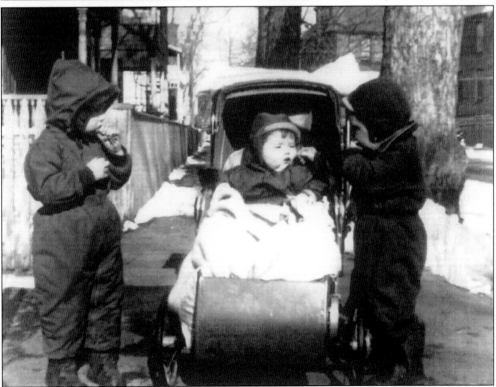

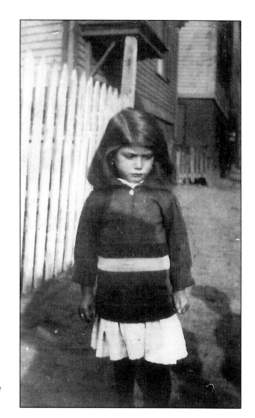

A very unhappy Mary Ruggieri on East Central Street and Dublin Court in 1917. She obviously did not want her picture taken.

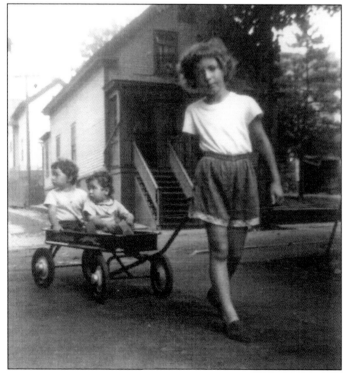

Barbara and Jacqueline Randall cruising down Winslow Street with N. Lamoureau at the wheel. (Scott Randall)

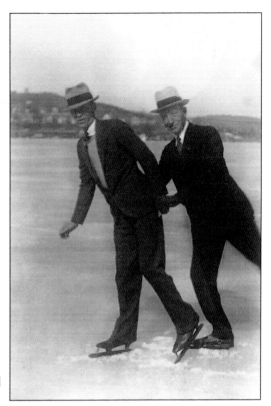

Emil Johnson leading his son Arthur on the ice at Indian Lake in the 1920s. Emil was a fireman for the city at Hose Company 9 and Engine Company 8. (Nancy Johnson)

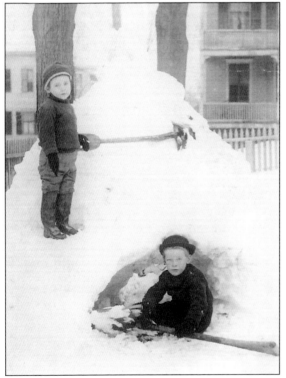

Arthur Johnson and his brother Everett (who became a city councilman in Ward 2), are seen here playing in the snow after a snowstorm that cancelled school. Those innocent faces make you wonder just what they are up to. In the background is a three-decker house. Because of the increased population due to immigration, more housing was necessary and three-deckers seemed to be the right solution at the time. (Nancy Johnson)

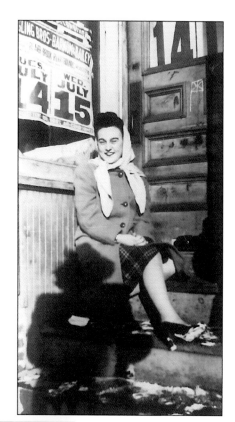

Irene Verdini, sitting on the stairs outside
the Silverio Family Store in 1942. It
appears that the circus was coming to town
on July 14 and 15. (Donna Murphy)

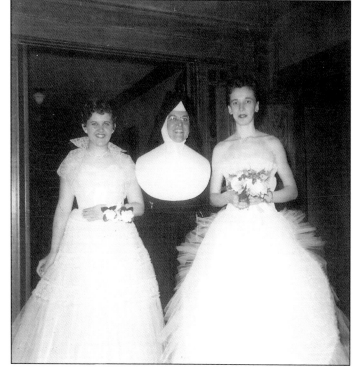

Prom night at St.
Stephen's School
in 1957. Diane
Kwiatkowski is on the
right and her friend
is to the left of Sister?
(Harriet Alukas)

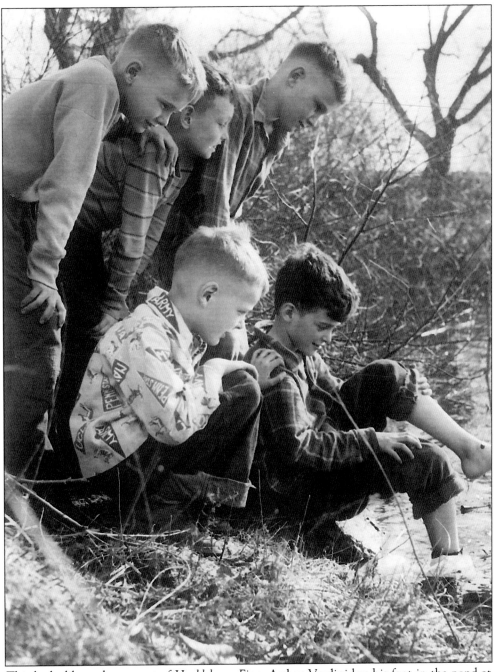

This looks like a chapter out of *Huckleberry Finn*. Arthur Verdini has his foot in the pond at Burncoat Park while the Ware brothers and O. Kelley look on. (Arthur Verdini/*Worcester Telegram & Gazette*)

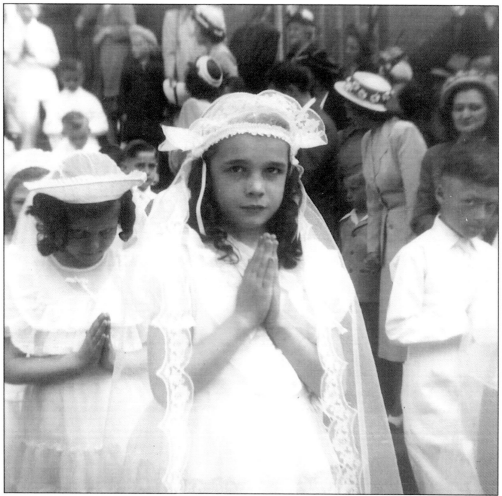

It is First Communion Sunday at St. John's Church on Temple Street and seven-year-old Tanya Kwiatkowski in her First Communion dress and veil walks angelically with her classmates outside the church. (Tanya Vasalofsky)

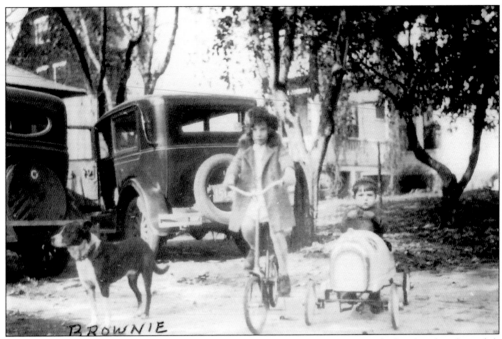

Brownie, the family dog, waits patiently for six-year-old Mary Louise Phelps (on her bicycle) and her four-year-old brother Windsor (in his pedal car). They both look anxious to start moving down Monroe Avenue. (Scott Randall)

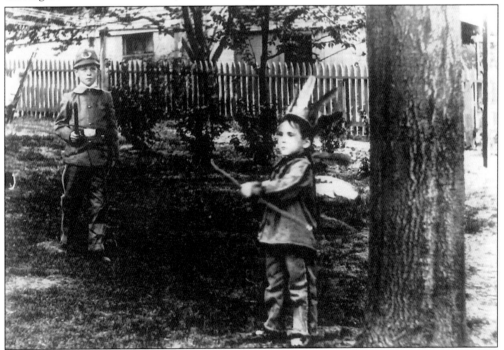

This photograph is of the Johnson brothers playing outside on Hollywood Street. The weather seems warm and the game is old—Everett is the Indian and Arthur is the soldier. (Nancy Johnson)

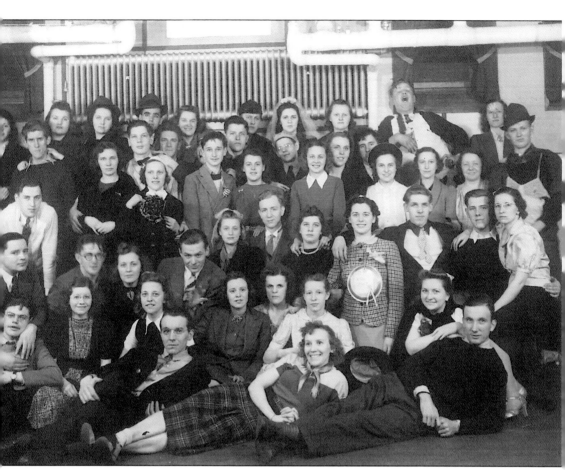

The Junior Knights of Lithuania—Council 26. (Michael Kamendulis)

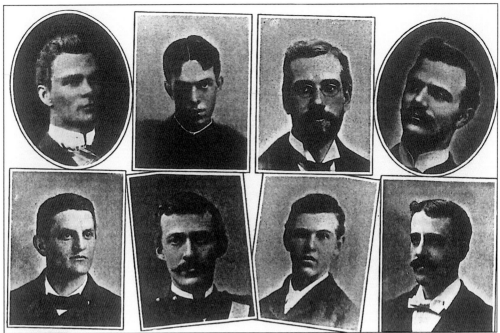

Childhood games sometimes become a harsh reality: shown are members of the Worcester Light Infantry who lost their lives as a result of the Spanish War. From left to right are: (bottom row) H. Wentworth, W. Roberts, J. Wheeler, and J. King; (top row) F. Taft, R. Dowse, A. Strewart, and S. Mayo.

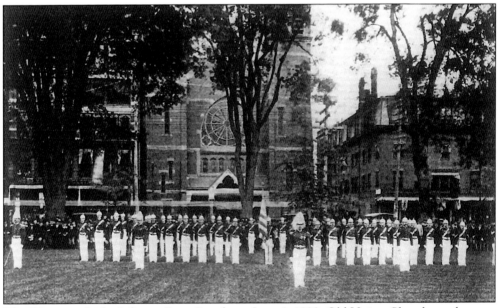

The Worcester Light Infantry Dress Parade on June 6, 1893. Old Union Church can be seen in the rear, on the corner of Commercial and Front Streets (where Sherer's once stood). The old Brewer Drugstore was on the opposite corner.

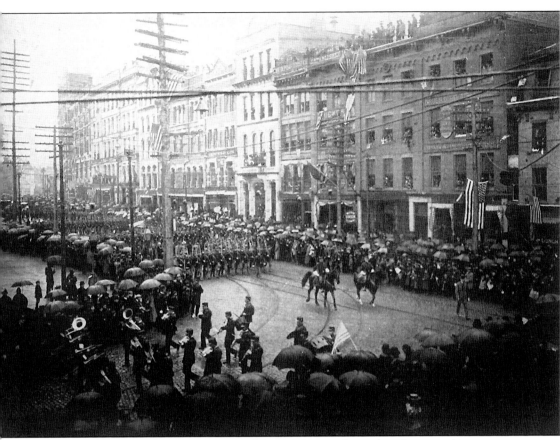

Although Tuesday, May 3, 1898, was a miserable day, thousands stood under rainy skies to say goodbye to Companies A, C, and H, which were on their way to Cuba.

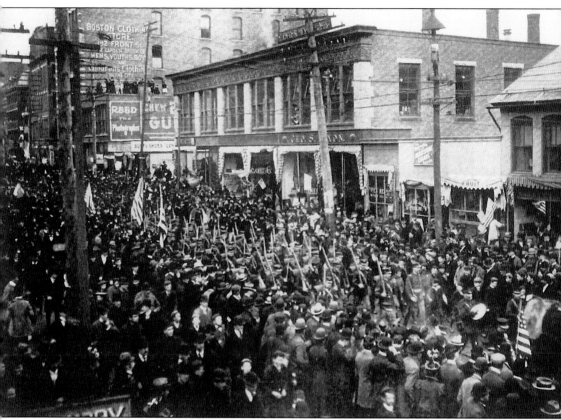

On May 4, 1898, the "Emmets" marched down Front Street before departing for Cuba, a day after Companies A, C, and H. Front Street had never before held as many people as it did that morning. The police had a difficult job clearing the way for the departing soldiers.

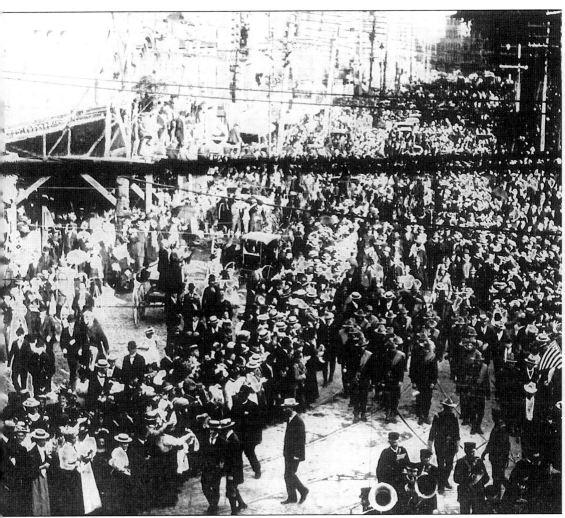

After the Spanish-American War was over Companies A, C, and H returned on October 31, 1898, to a reception worthy of their services. Schools closed early that day and businesses shut down for the duration of the parade. Later that evening the veterans were honored at Mechanics Hall.

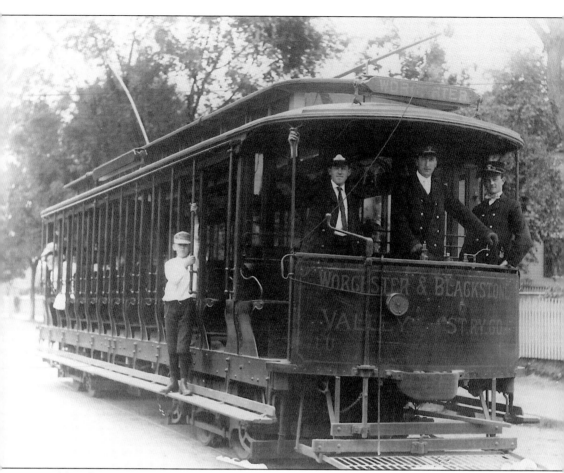

After the war, men returned to work as usual—to jobs such as conducting on the trolley cars.

Three

Schools and Sports

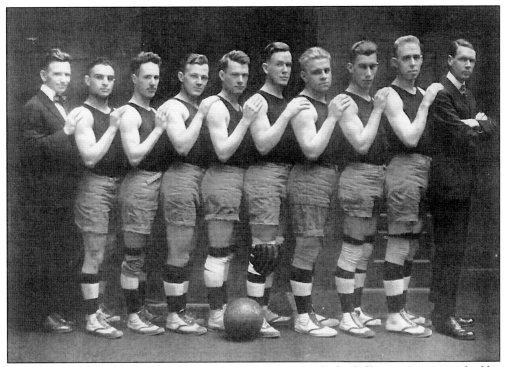

In 1918 Worcester Polytechnic Institute had its first varsity basketball team. It was coached by R. Ward, managed by R. Tenney, and led by its captain, J. Kushner.

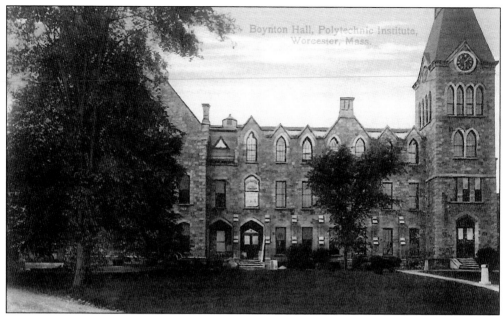

Worcester Polytechnic Institute is the third oldest private engineering college in the nation. It was created in 1865, when John Boynton founded the Worcester Free Institution of Industrial Science. Mr. Boynton and Ichabod Washburn endowed the first two buildings on campus, Boynton Hall and Washburn Shops.

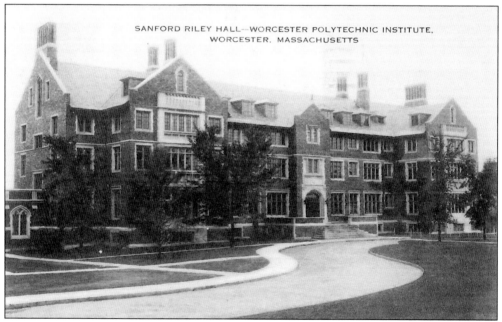

At the south end of the Quad stands Stanford-Riley Hall. Mrs. Katharine Higgins Riley, daughter of Milton Higgins (a former superintendent of the Washburn Shops), bequeathed her home and property to the school, hoping it would become a student center. Since 1927 it has been the home of many freshmen.

54

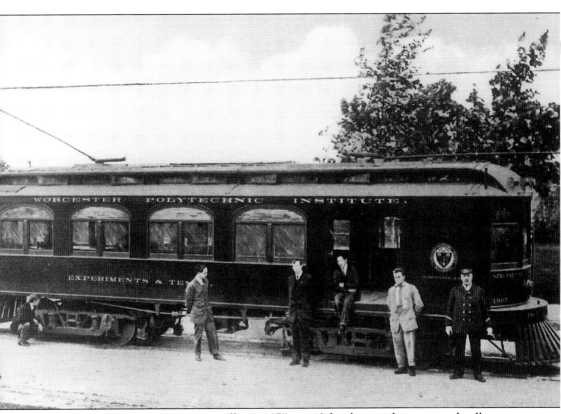

The Worcester Polytechnic Institute's trolley "1907" was 40 feet long and was painted pullman green with gold trimmings. It had side and end doors but no regular steps, and was equipped to automatically test various characteristics of the trolley rails: voltage, current, the resistance of railbonds, and other things which one engineer said "it would take a Philadelphia lawyer to understand." This car tested thousands of miles of track on the networks of New England's electric railways before being scrapped in 1928.

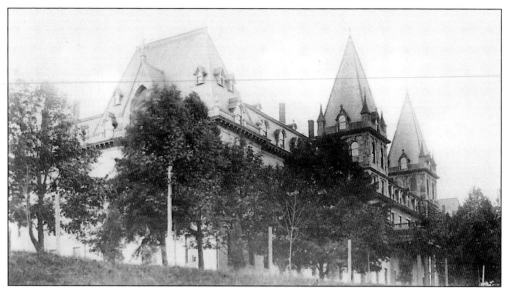

Holy Cross College was founded in 1843 by Bishop Fenwick. It is the oldest Catholic college in New England and the third oldest in the country.

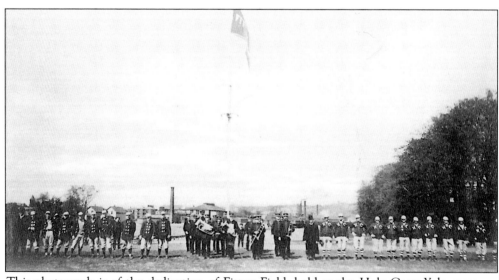

This photograph is of the dedication of Fitton Field, held at the Holy Cross-Yale game on May 20, 1905.

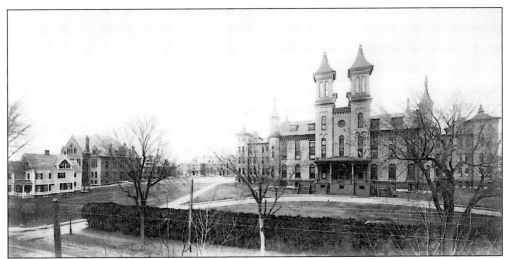

Worcester Academy is one of the nation's oldest preparatory schools. The most prominent building on campus is Davis Hall, named after Isaac Davis. Built in 1852 to accommodate the Worcester Medical College, it was used as a military hospital during the Civil War. It eventually served as a dormitory until the 1960s.

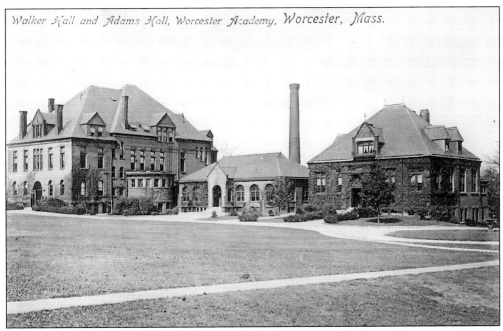

Walker Hall and Adams Hall, Worcester Academy, Worcester, Mass.

Walker Hall and Adams Hall were later added to the campus. The first of the major additions was Walker Hall, the main administration building, which was dedicated in 1890; Adams Hall was built in 1893 and served as the dining facility. Across the Quad is the Warner Memorial Theatre. The theatre was a gift from Harry Warner, president of Warner Brothers Pictures, in memory of his son Lewis, a member of the class of 1928.

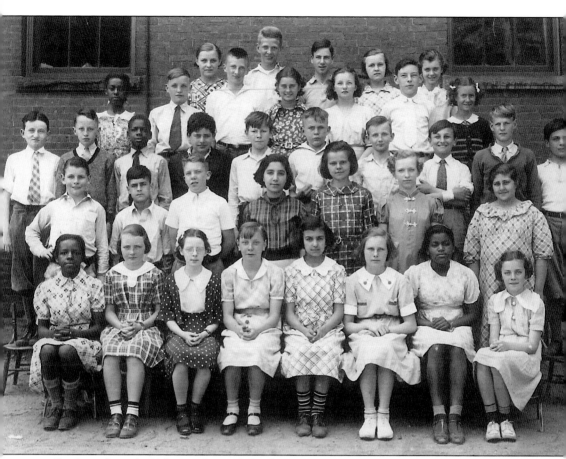

Students from the Belmont Street School pose on May 29, 1936. From left to right are: (first row) M. Kelly, A. McKinney, A. Murray, H. Sarta, E. Glanian, F. Falkengrin, B. Cangdon, and L. Resndo; (second row) W. Rouke, G. Soter, J. Riely, N. Shanigan, M. Brennan, E. Johnson, and A. Silverio; (third row) J. Murphy, D. Clauson, H. Kelly, T. Silverlo, H. Strafford, E. Enos, E. Eaton, E. Golia, E. Skog, and J. Franklin; (fourth row) S. Rainy, R. Cole, R. Burgess, L. Carter, A. Johnson, R. Gagnon, and B. Gillis; (fifth row) J. Smith, V. Hill, W. Jones, H. Tuomi, and J. Hayden. (Donna Murphy)

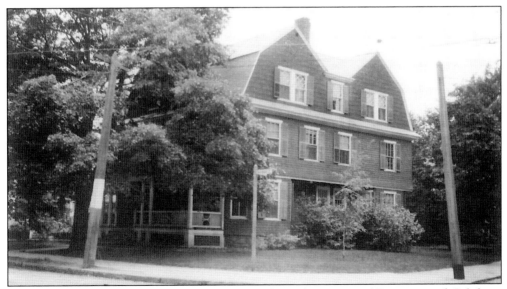

Worcester Grammar Schools

This is to Certify That *Arthur Verdini*

a member of the

Belmont Street Grammar School

has completed the prescribed Grammar School Course of Study, and is entitled to admission to the High School.

Given by the School Committee

Worcester, Mass. *1-24-29*

Principal

Visiting Committee

A grammar school diploma earned by Arthur Verdini from the Belmont Street School, dated January 24, 1929.

The Phi Gamma Delta fraternity house, located on the corner of Boynton and Salisbury Streets. This Pi Iota chapter was established on November 20, 1891, and is the oldest fraternity at Worcester Polytechnic Institute.

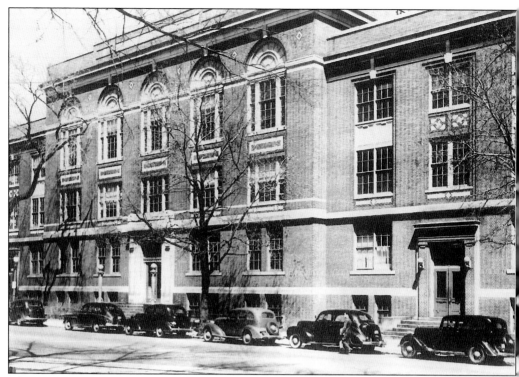

The Worcester Boys Trade High School was established in 1909 at Armory Square. It was one of the first trade schools in Massachusetts and for several years was one of the largest in New England. It was founded by Milton Higgins, who became one of the chief advocates of trade schools throughout the region. (Donna Murphy)

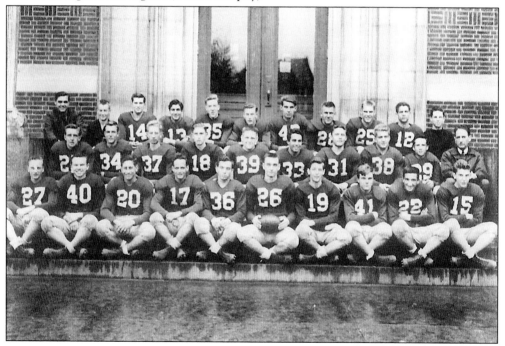

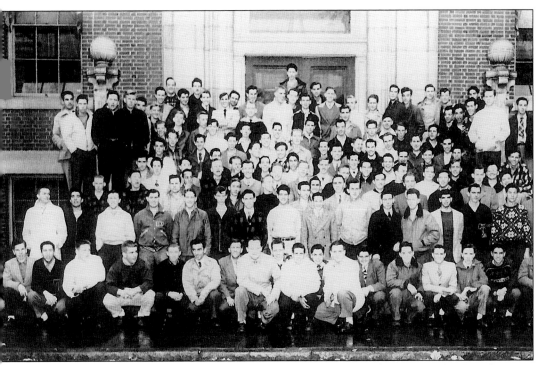

Gathered in front of the main building of the Worcester Boys Trade High School is the graduating class of 1948. (Donna Murphy)

Opposite: The Worcester Boys Trade High School football team of 1947. (Donna Murphy)

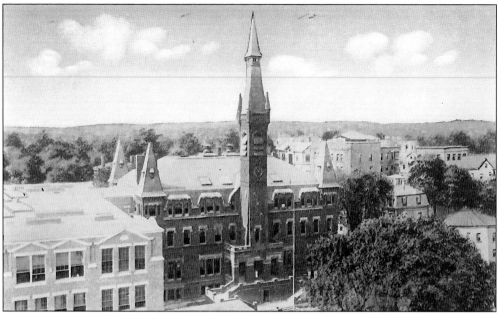

This building on the corner of Chatham and Irving Streets was originally Commerce High School, but is now called the School Administration Building. The high school was eventually moved to Walnut Street, and the class of 1966 was the last graduating class before the building on Walnut Street was razed to make way for the Paul Revere Insurance Company.

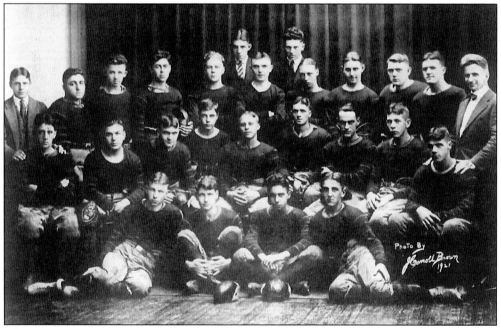

The 1922 Commerce High School championship football team. From left to right are: (first row) Ross, Carney, Cardinal, and Savage; (second row) Landers, Franklin, Dudley, Bishop, Eld (captain), D. Healy, Burnham, Montgomery, and H. Healy; (third row) Peterson (manager), Abodeely, Shea, Doherty, Nelson, Clifford, Arnott, Lynch, Hussey, Putnam, and Mr. Ward (coach); (fourth row) Ryan and Messier.

TO COMMERCE

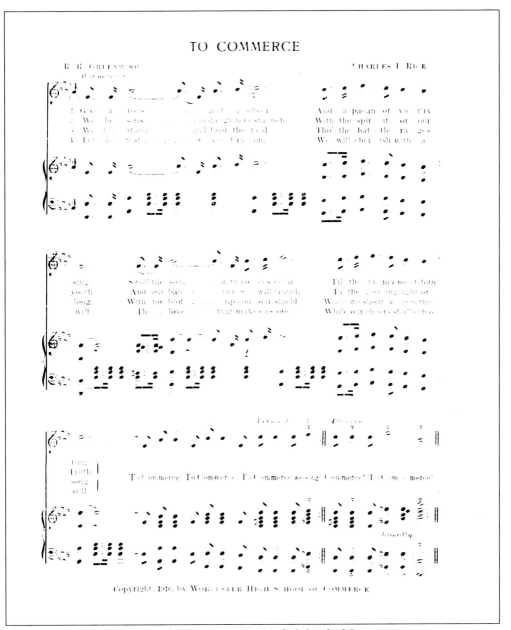

This song was written in 1916 by the Worcester High School of Commerce.

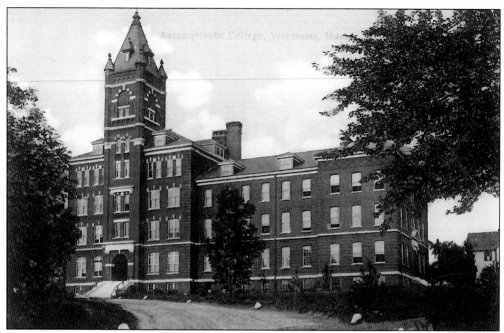

The Assumptionist Fathers established America's first Franco-American college in 1904: Assumption College. On June 9, 1953, a tornado swept through Worcester and tore off the top story of the main building. This disaster was overcome, however, when the college rebuilt a more spacious and modern campus on Salisbury Street. After Assumption Prep closed, the campus became the home of Quinsigamond Community College.

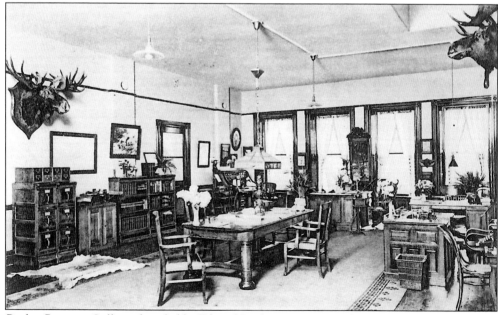

Becker Business College, founded by Edward Becker in 1887, was located on Front Street. Mr. Becker saw the need for trained personnel in business and as a result began a business college.

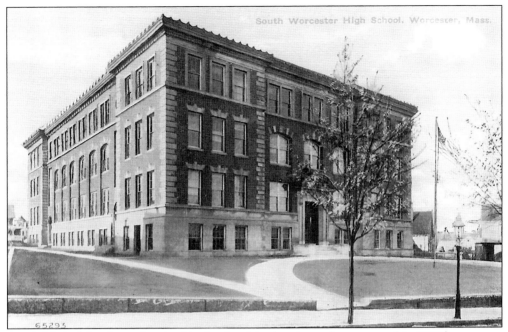

South High School was the third high school in the city and was erected in 1900/1 at a cost of $180,000. The brick building, located on Richards Street, is three stories high and houses twenty-three classrooms.

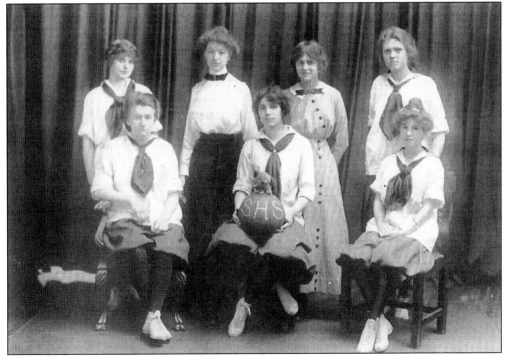

The South High School girls' basketball team of 1913.

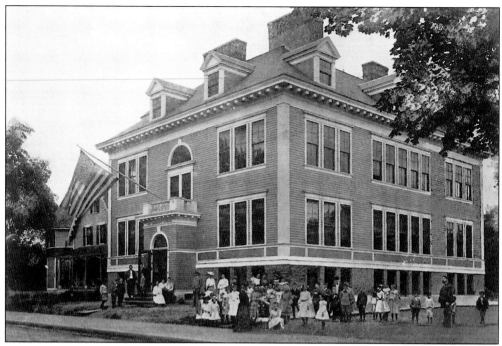

The Bancroft School was named in honor of George Bancroft, the renowned historian. The grammar grades were for both boys and girls, but the high school was at one time for girls only.

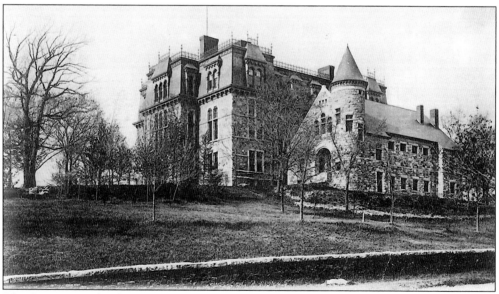

The State Normal School opened on September 15, 1874. Located on St. Anne's Hill, the school trained and prepared young women and men to become teachers. Beginning in 1915, admission was restricted to women only; in 1932 the school relocated and was renamed the Worcester State Teachers College, and in 1940 men were again allowed to apply as students.

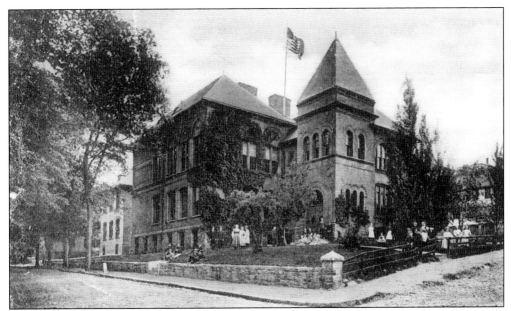

Since 1910, the Elizabeth Street Elementary School has been associated with the Normal School, which has allowed the younger students to benefit from the Normal School's excellent teaching staff.

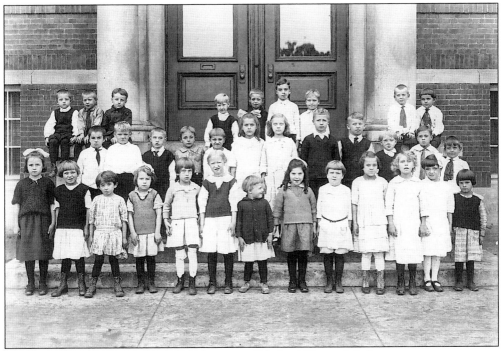

The Ward Street School class of 1922 picture. (Michael Kamendulis)

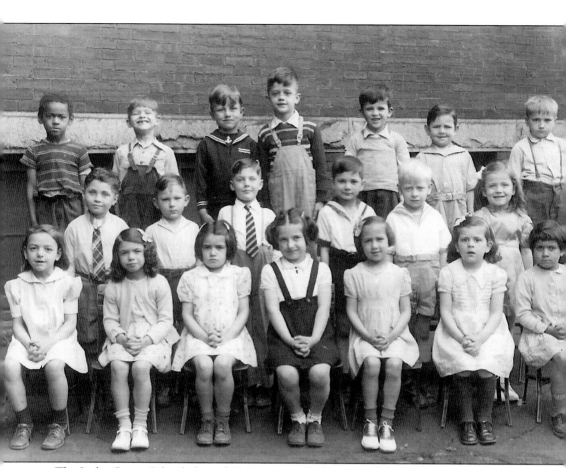

The Ledge Street School class of 1943 picture. (Bob Vasalofsky)

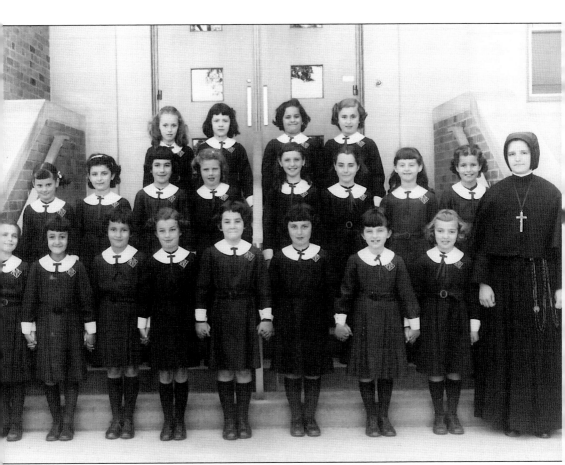

Students of the Venerini Academy in the 1950s. The uniforms were wool with a stiff collar and cuffs. Those identified are: L. Tedesco, P. Flaherty, D. Coppola, L. Verdini, L. Batista, L. Marchese, M. Quinlan, P. Bombredi, N. Stubbert, J. Carlantuono, R. Martin, M. Marchese, and F. DiCiccio. The teacher is Sister Marie Doloris.

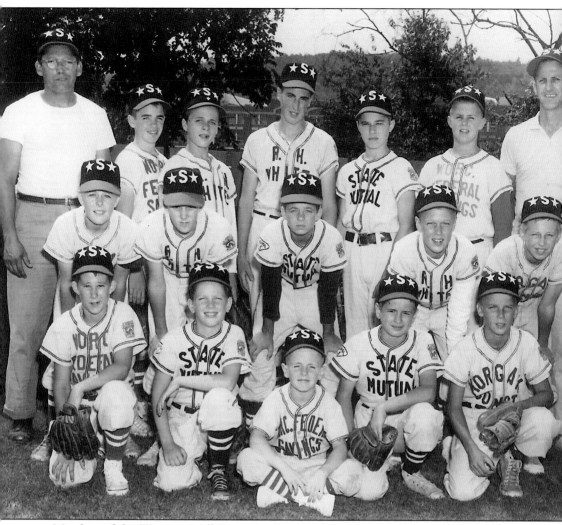

Members of the Worcester All Star team. From left to right are: (first row) Mike Dodd, Jack Shea, Whitey Gillis, Earl Sherrer, and unknown; (second row) unknown, unknown, Paul O'Brien, Chipper Morgan, and unknown; (third row) Leo Wickson, Jack Gillis, unknown, Bill Hurley, Randy Gould, Tom Yeulenski, and Anthony Yeulenski, Sr.

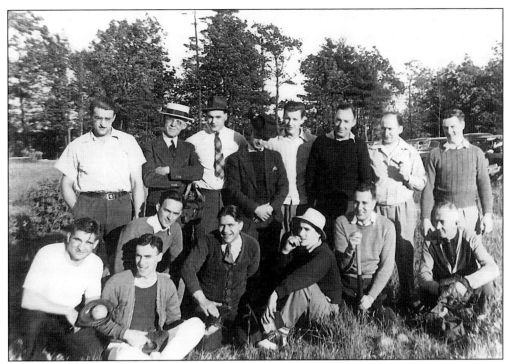

These gentlemen appear ready for a softball game. (Michael Kamendulis)

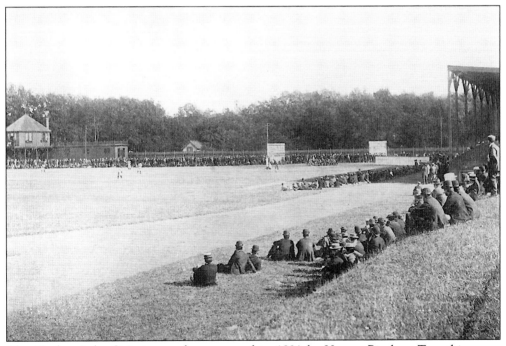

The Oval at Lake Quinsigamond was opened in 1891 by Horace Bigelow. Two things are worthy of note in this picture: the number of spectators dressed in their Sunday clothes, and the absence of women in the crowd.

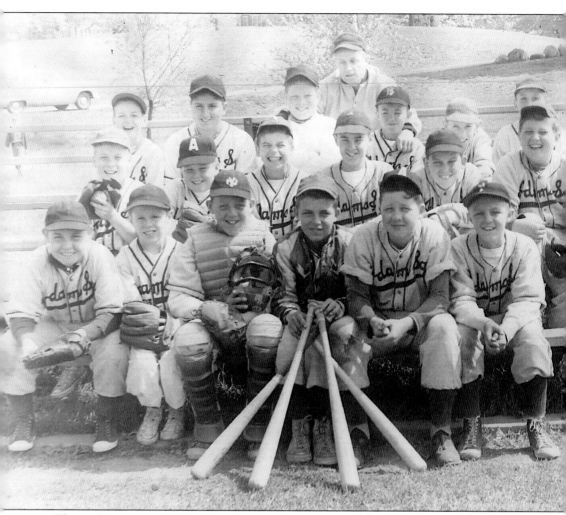

These athletes were the Northern Section Champions in May 1956 and the City Champions in June 1956. From left to right are: (first row) E. Sloan, D. Griffin, W. Russell, D. Benoit (captain), R. Howe, and J. Paul; (second row) J. Kennedy, D. Crockett, P. McCann, A. Baribeault, B. Gervais, and J. White; (third row) C. Conway, B. Anispigean, B. Daly, J. Donohue, J. Howe, and B. Deering; (fourth row) Eddie Bates (coach).

Four

Parks and Entertainment

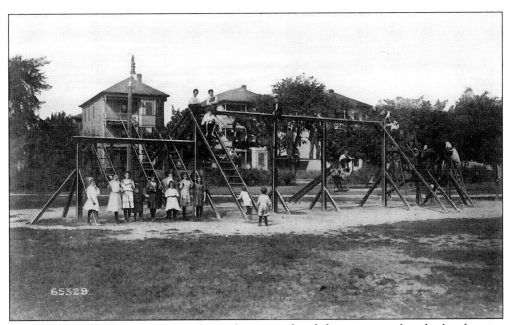

The playgrounds at Crompton Park on the east side of the city were bought by the city for $60,000.

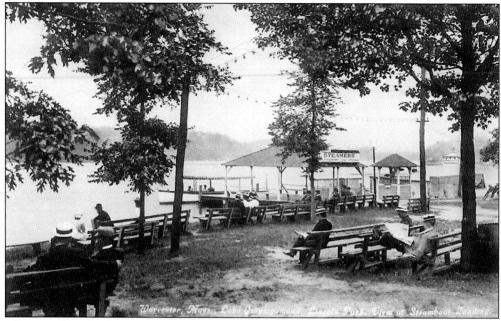

The steamboat landing at Lincoln Park on Lake Quinsigamond.

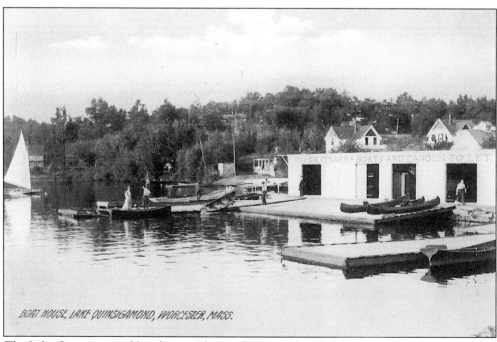

The Lake Quinsigamond boathouse. This is where couples of all ages would go to rent a canoe and spend a romantic afternoon together.

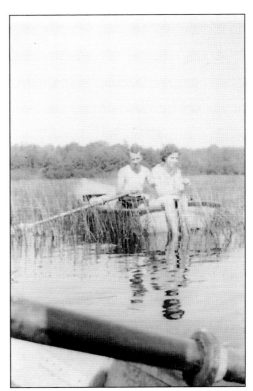

Francis Clark and Mary Ruggieri on Lake
Quinsigamond in 1935.

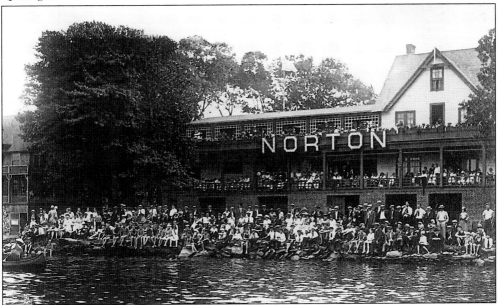

The Norton Boat Club on Lake Quinsigamond was organized just before the Depression and
lasted for only two years. The clubhouse was open to all employees and more than five hundred
took advantage of this opportunity. Full membership entitled them to weekly dances, parties
(such as this one), and winter carnivals. The Norton Crew team in this picture took part in the
Olympic trials in 1920 on Lake Quinsigamond. They were also the first to row their "blimps"
under the new Quinsigamond bridge. (James Magay)

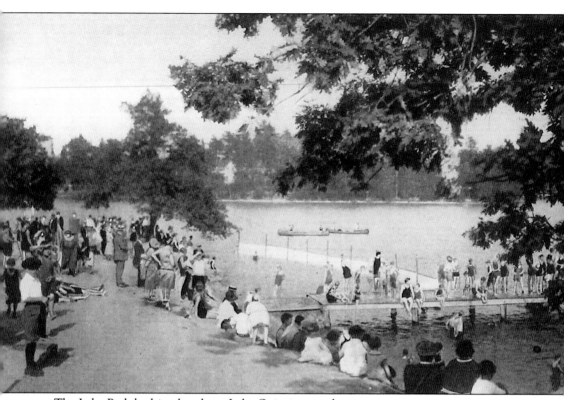

The Lake Park bathing beach on Lake Quinsigamond.

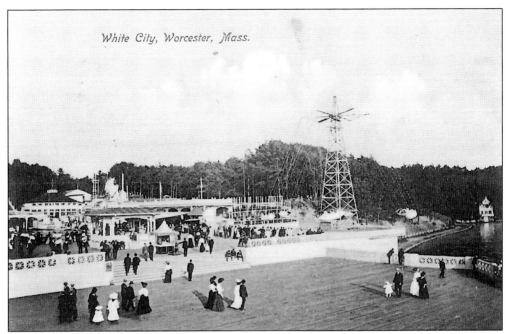

The White City Amusement Park on Lake Quinsigamond in 1907. Everyone is wearing hats—even the young girls. Do they really expect them to remain secure on these rides?

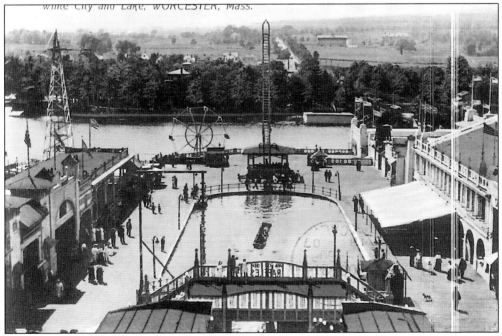

Another view of White City on the Lake. In the foreground, the inground pool apparently had two different purposes: it was used for both the log ride and the high dive.

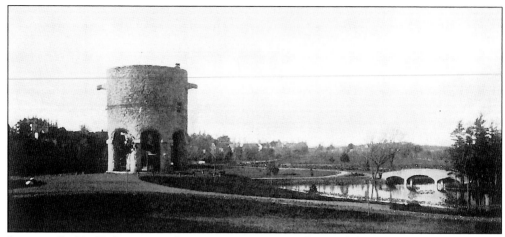

Institute Park's 30-foot tower drew many visitors. Stephen Salisbury III had this duplicate of an ancient tower built in 1892. It was called Worcester's Norse Tower because of the misconception that it was a replica of a tower built by Vikings.

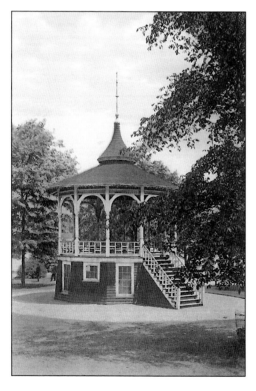

Institute Park's bandstand was a favorite place for band concerts, because there were many seats and it was possible for occupants of carriages to listen from the driveways.

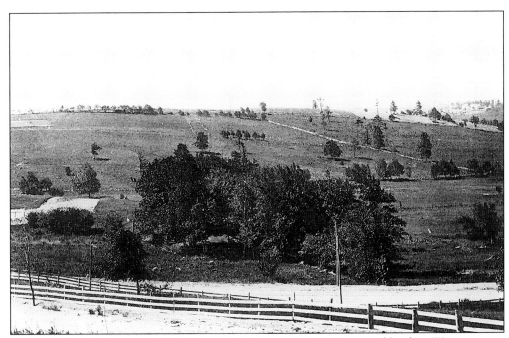

A view of Dodge Park in 1894. Thomas Dodge presented 13 acres of land to Worcester on September 27, 1890. This park at one time included a beautiful grove, a never-failing spring, and a large open field. It was one of the most attractive parks in the area.

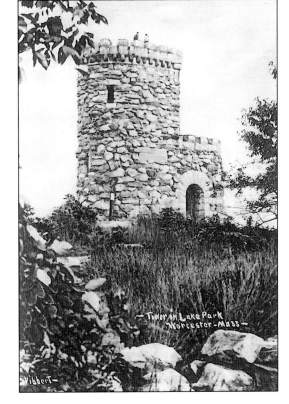

Lake Tower sits on the site of Samuel Lenorson's home. Lenorson's twelve-year-old son was kidnapped by Indians in 1695. On March 15, 1697, two Haverhill women were also kidnapped, but they joined forces with young Samuel Lenorson, Jr. and killed and scalped many of their abductors. They then managed to paddle down the Merrimac River to safety and return to their families.

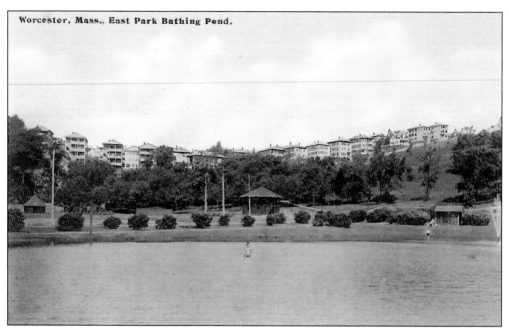

East Park, purchased for $50,000, contained 66 acres. It was originally called Chandler Hill Park. The small pond in the foreground is where children went "swimming." Bell Pond forms part of this park and at one time provided water for bathhouses.

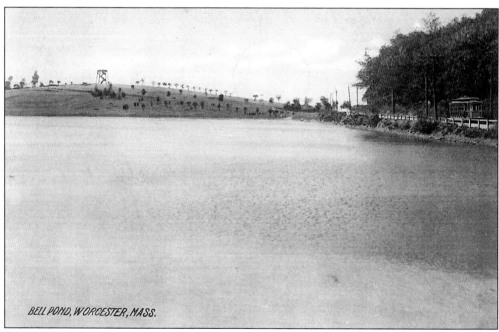

BELL POND, WORCESTER, MASS.

Bell Pond, formerly Bladder Pond, sits on the top of Belmont Hill. At one time a floating island sat in this pond, which the city removed at a cost of $2,758. It's name was given to it because of its resemblance to a giant bell.

80

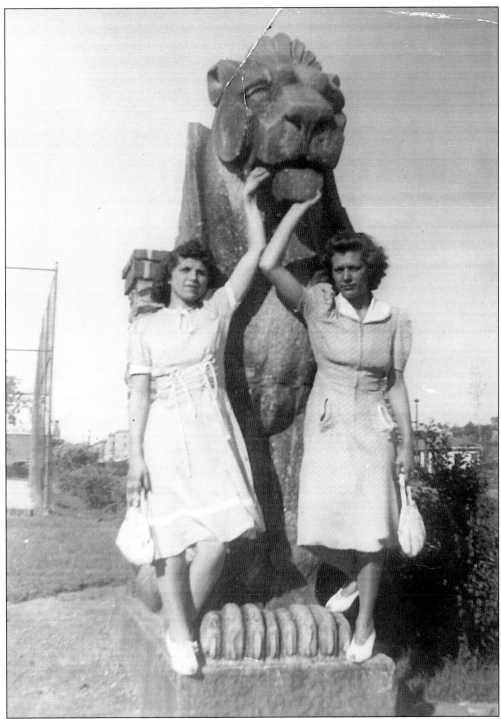

In front of East Park on Shrewsbury Street were the carved stone lions that for forty years supported the stone arch of old Union Station at Washington Square. Harriet Alukas and her friend seem to be trying to give the lions a helping hand. (Harriet Alukas)

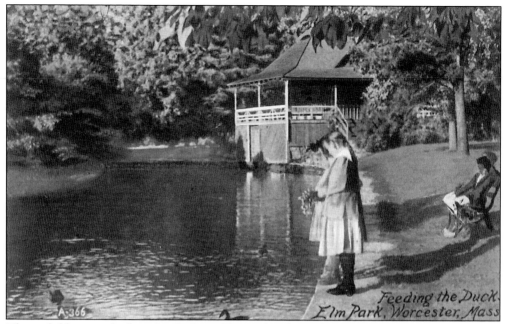

These children are feeding the ducks at Elm Park. This park was created in what is believed to have been the first purchase of land for use as a public park in the United States. At one time there was a deer park in the triangle between Highland Street, Park Avenue, and the path along the foot of Newton Hill.

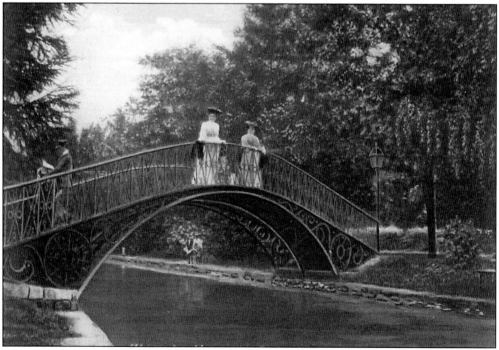

Elm Park displays flowering plants and shrubs from early spring until late autumn. The evergreens on Newton Hill afford an ideal background for the older part of the park, which was purchased in 1854 (Newton Hill became part of Elm Park in 1888).

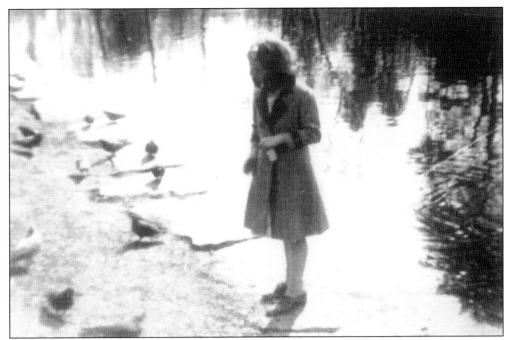

Mary Louise Phelps feeding the pigeons at Elm Park around 1940. (Scott Randall)

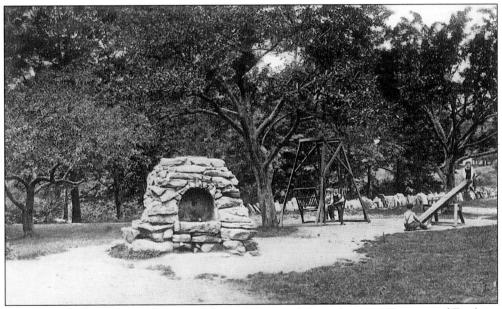

Greenwood Park, purchased in 1905, lies on Greenwood Street between Tatman and Forsberg Streets and consists of 14.9 acres. This park was one of the few chosen to be a city playground in 1910, with a director and a staff of paid and volunteer assistants.

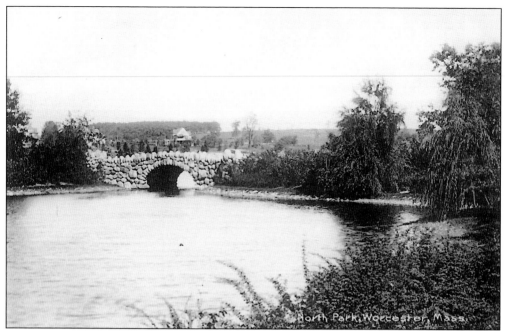

North Park, more commonly known as Burncoat Park, was created from 41 acres of land purchased from various private citizens. Its pathways and walks were some of the most attractive to flower lovers. Ice skating was an annual event here in the winter as was tennis in the summer. Now the expressway runs through the park and the tennis courts, flowers, and stone bridge are gone forever.

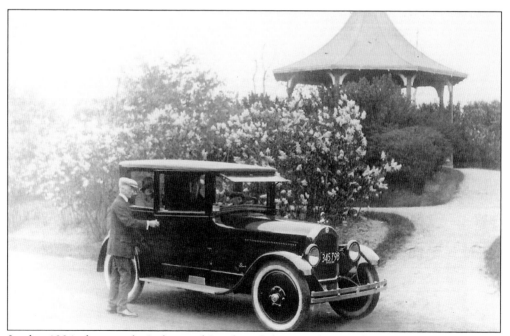

In this 1924 photograph Arthur and Ingeborg Johnson, along with Mrs. Emil Johnson, are parked next to flowering lilac bushes near the pavilion. (Nancy Johnson)

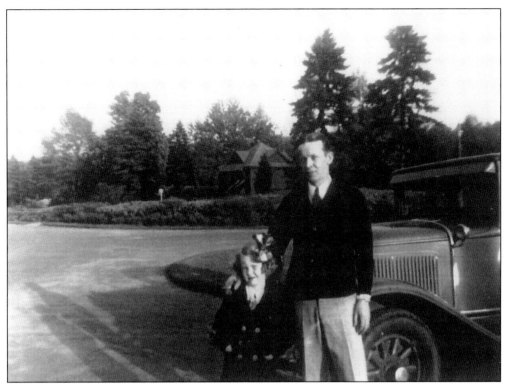

Nancy Johnson standing with her father Arthur at Burncoat Park. The manicured grounds are beautiful. (Nancy Johnson)

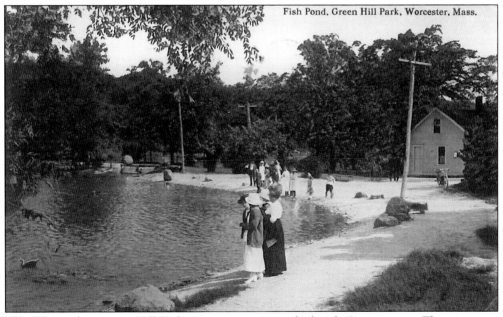

Fish Pond, Green Hill Park, Worcester, Mass.

The fish pond at Green Hill Park was at one time stocked with German carp. The city came into possession of the Green estate in 1905 for $54,900, a mere fraction of its value.

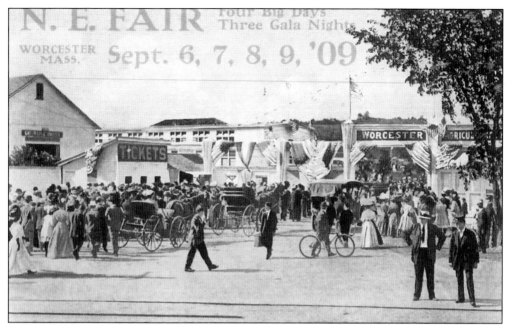

The Worcester Agricultural Fairgrounds on West Boylston Street near Greendale were the site of the New England Fair. These fairs were always one of the greatest events of the year and for over half a century they drew huge crowds.

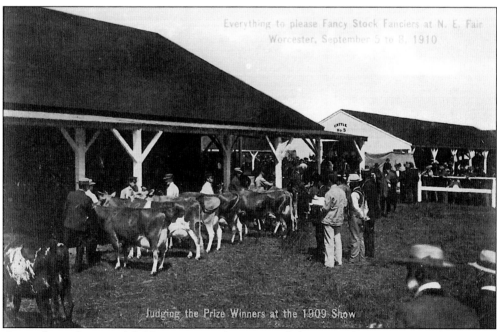

Cows, sheep, hogs, and field crops were always on exhibition at the New England Fair. The fairs went out of existence in 1930, after 111 years of continuous activity.

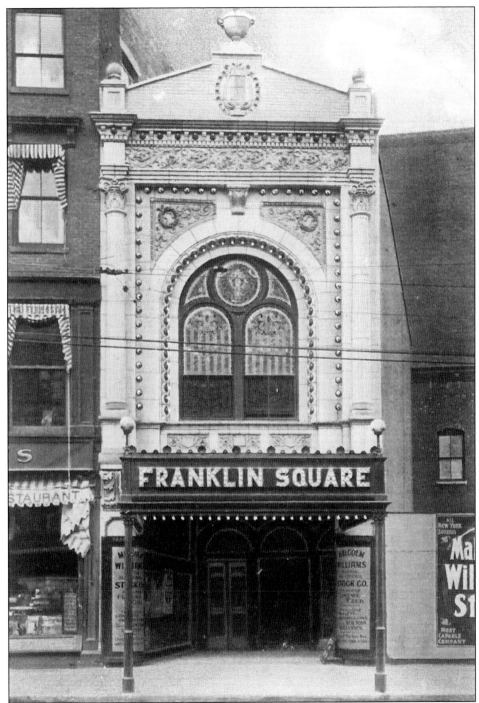

Franklin Theatre, later called the Grand Theatre, was purchased by Mr. Poli from the Taylor estate. Since that time, it has been the home of Poli's stock companies nearly every year. At other times it has been in various circuits of traveling companies. Some of the best sensational drama plays can be seen here, and where others have failed, Mr. Poli has had crowded houses. He has made all three of his large theatres very profitable.

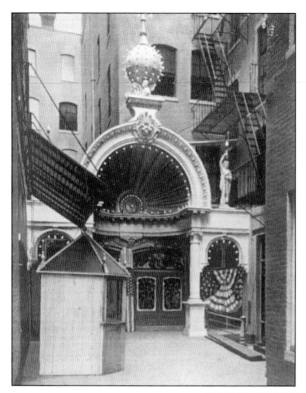

C.Z. Poli purchased the Crompton Block on Mechanic Street after it was destroyed by fire in March 1905. He remodeled it into a theatre, opened an entrance on Front Street, and presented the "only the best" vaudeville to the people of Worcester.

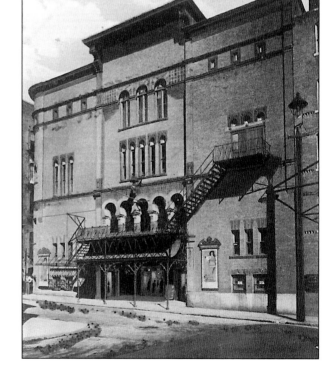

The Worcester Theatre on Exchange Street was patronized by the well-to-do exclusively. Before the days of motion pictures, Worcester was visited by some of the best theatrical companies in the country, and the Worcester Theatre thrived between 1890 and 1910.

WORCESTER THEATRE

MONDAY NIGHT, MAY 17 ~~19 15~~

WILLIAM A. BRADY PRESENTS

ROBERT B. MANTELL

IN SHAKESPEAREAN AND CLASSIC PLAYS

KING JOHN

By WILLIAM SHAKESPEARE

THE CAST

KING JOHN ....MR. MANTELL
Prince Henry, Son to the King..............................Miss Virginia Bronson
Arthur, Duke of Bretagne, Nephew to the King.............................
                     Miss Genevieve Hamper
The Lord Bigot..Mr. Edward Lewers
Hubert de Burgh...Mr. John Burke
Robert Faulconbridge, Son to Sir Robert Faulconbridge.................
                     Mr. Francis Macleod
Philip, the Bastard, his Half-Brother............................Mr. Fritz Leiber
Philip, King of France.......................................Mr. Walter Gibbs
Louis, the Dauphin...Mr. Guy Lindsley
Lymoges, Duke of Austria......................................Mr. Harold Skinner
Cardinal Pandulph, the Pope's Legate. ....Mr. Frank Peters
The Earl of Pembroke..Mr. Harry Howard
The Earl of Essex...Mr. Charles Keene
The Earl of Salisbury...Mr. John Gibbs
Chatillon, Ambassador from France to King John...........Mr. John Gibbs
A Knight..Mr. Edwin Foos
A Citizen of Angiers..Mr. Edward Lewers
Second Attendant..Mr. Charles Reasoner
Queen Elinor, Mother to King John................Miss Genevieve Reynolds
Constance, Mother to Arthur......................................Miss Florence Auer
Blanche of Spain, Niece to King John.........................Miss Ethel Mantell

PLACE OF ACTION

ACT I.—Setting, England. A Room of State in King John's Palace.
ACT II.—Setting, France. Before the Walls of Angiers.
ACT III.—Setting 1, The same. The French King's Tent. Setting 2,
    The Plains near Angiers. Setting 3, The French King's
    Tent.
ACT IV.—Setting, Northampton. A Room in the Castle.
ACT V.—Setting, England. Throne Room in King John's Palace.
ACT VI.—Setting, Before the Castle.
ACT VII.—Setting, 1, An Open Place in the Neighborhood of Swins-
    stead Abbe. Setting 2, The Orchard of Swinstead Abbey.

TUESDAY EVENING, MAY 18

WILLIAM A. BRADY PRESENTS

ROBERT B. MANTELL

IN SHAKESPEAREAN AND CLASSIC PLAYS

MACBETH

This presentation of *King John* was staged at the Worcester Theatre on May 17, 1915.

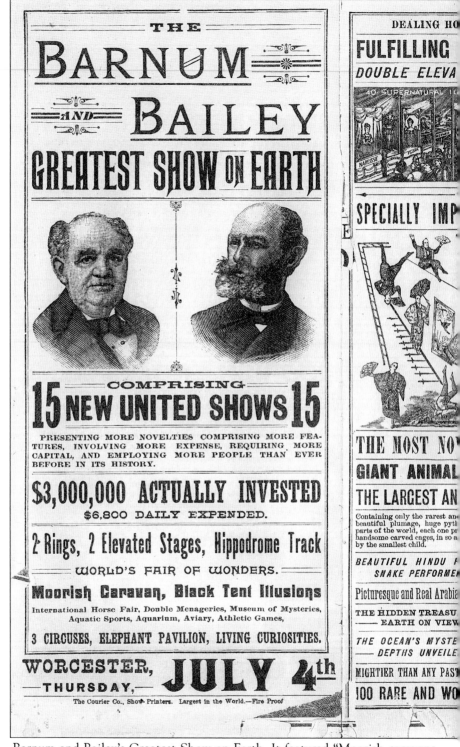

Barnum and Bailey's Greatest Show on Earth. It featured "Moorish caravans, the smallest, strangest, and most intelligent of all elephants, primitive

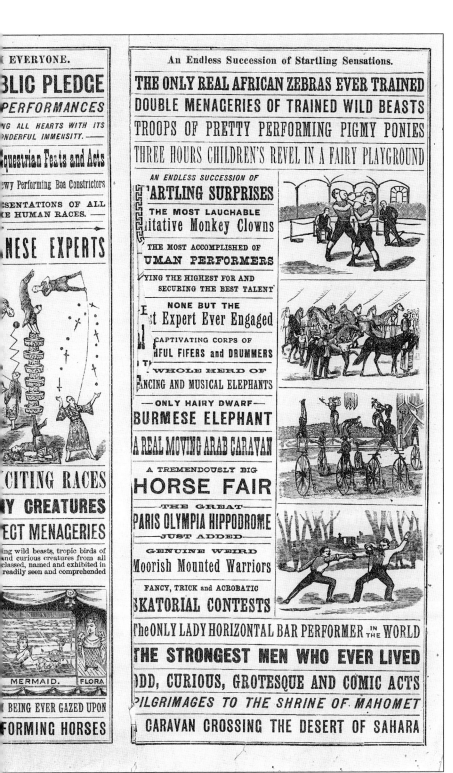

Africans, real Bedouins, genuine Moors, and native African dances and much more."

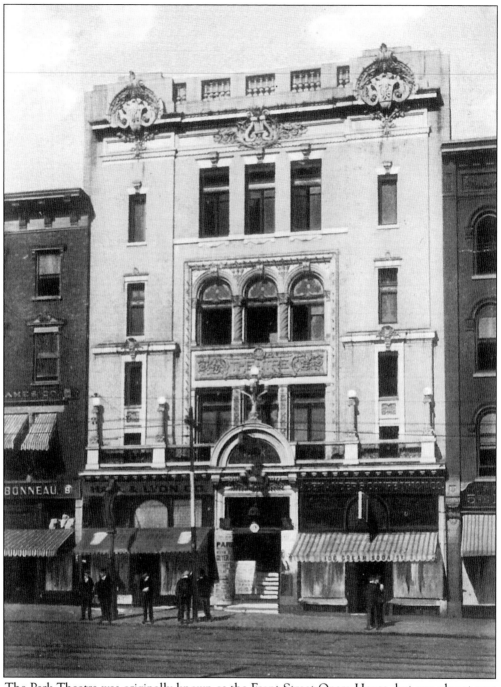

The Park Theatre was originally known as the Front Street Opera House, but was also at one point the Bijou Theatre.

Five

Buildings

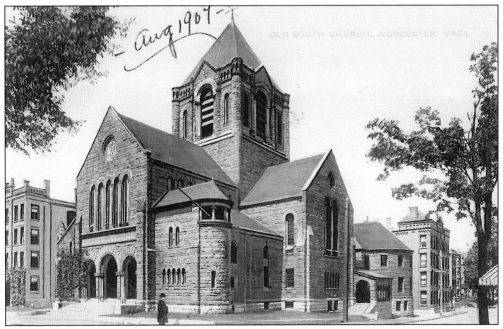

On the corner of Main and Wellington Streets stood the new Old South Church. The bell cast by Paul Revere hung in the belfry. This building, built in 1898, replaced Worcester's historic Old South Church.

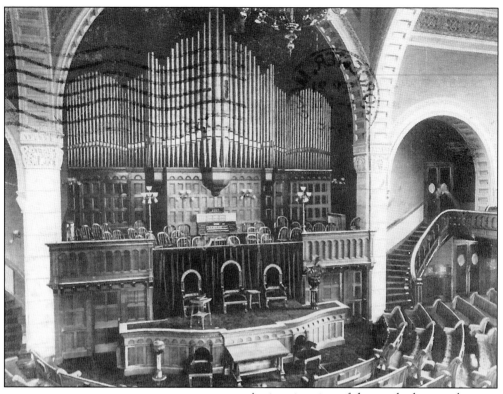

An interior view of the newly decorated auditorium of the new Old South Church.

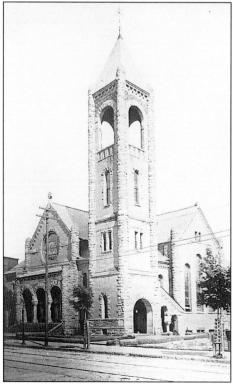

Pilgrim Church began with a Sunday school service on May 13, 1883, in the home of Mrs. Fannie H. Mighill.

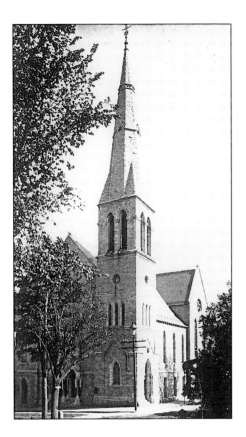

Plymouth Church was located on the corner of Pearl and Chestnut Streets. On April 15, 1869, fourteen young men decided to form a new Congregational church; the result, after they gathered some financial backing, was Plymouth Church.

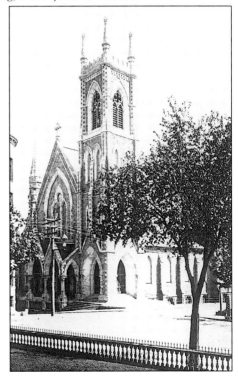

St. Paul's Church was located on the corner of Chatham and High Streets. Father Power, then pastor of St. Anne's Church, bought the land for $15,000 in August 1866. At a meeting in January 1867, Catholics subscribed $7,100 to a building fund and ground was broken for the new church in the spring of 1868.

St. Anne's Church began on Shrewsbury Street. Father Power built a small rectory on Shrewsbury Street in 1863, and that humble structure remained in use until 1885. On September 5, 1882, the site of the new St. Anne's was bought from the Worcester Lunatic Asylum for $10,685. The cornerstone was laid on June 15, 1884, and the first Mass was held in the basement on October 11, 1885. The new church was a Gothic structure that seated 1,150 people. In 1891 a spacious rectory was built at the rear of the building.

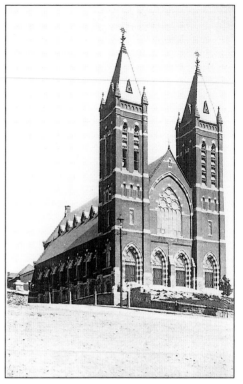

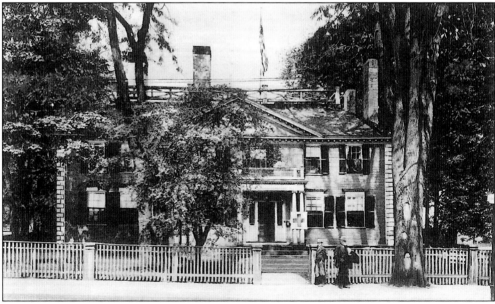

Salisbury Mansion was built in 1770 on the north side of Lincoln Square. Stephen Salisbury originally bought the land from the Honorable John Hancock, and lived there until his death in 1829. Madam Salisbury (as she was called) kept the mansion in the family, and it was often the scene of social gatherings, for she was known for her hospitality. After her death, the house was used as a private school and was later moved to the corner of Lancaster Street and Institute Road.

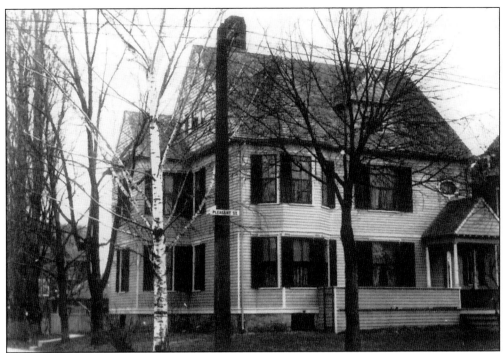

A 1920 photograph of the home of Dr. Onley D. and Marion (Houghton) Phelps at 743 Pleasant Street. (Scott Randall)

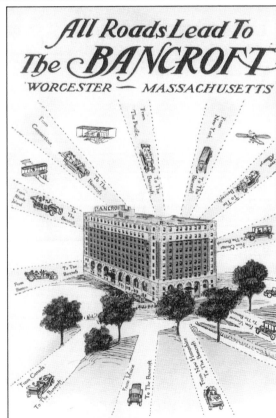

A Bancroft Hotel advertisement declaring that all roads lead to the Bancroft Hotel.

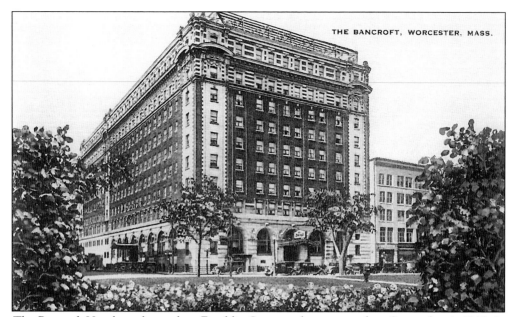

The Bancroft Hotel was located on Franklin Street and was opened on September 1, 1913. It contained accommodations for 320 guests, and the total cost of the building and furnishings was $1,250,000. Named in honor of George Bancroft, a bust of this distinguished man was placed in the main lobby.

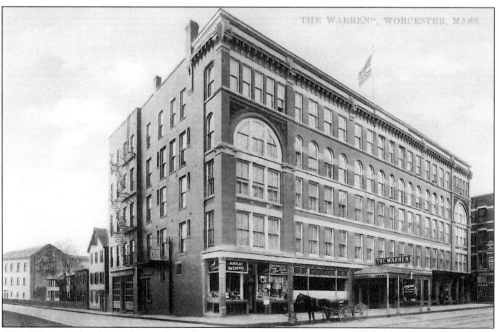

The Warren Hotel was located on Front Street. In 1916 rooms with baths were $2 and up, while rooms without baths were only $1.50 and up.

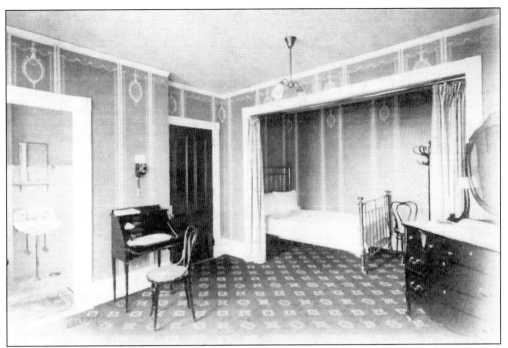

This photograph shows a typical suite at the Warren Hotel. The brass bed is set back in an alcove, and the marbletop bureau and secretary desk are in the main room.

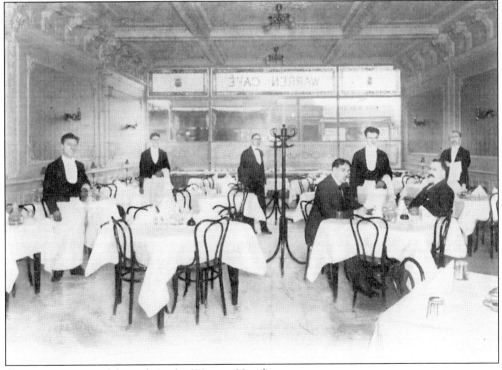

An interior view of the cafe in the Warren Hotel.

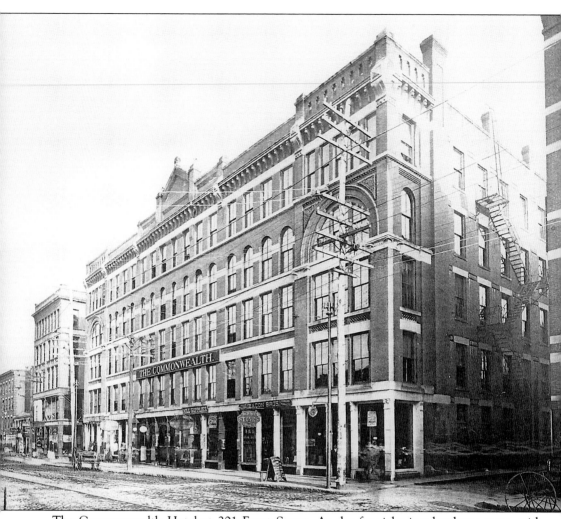

The Commonwealth Hotel at 201 Front Street. At the far right is a hardware store, with shovels in the window and a carriage in the front of the store. Judging from the amount of activity going on, it was a slow day in downtown Worcester.

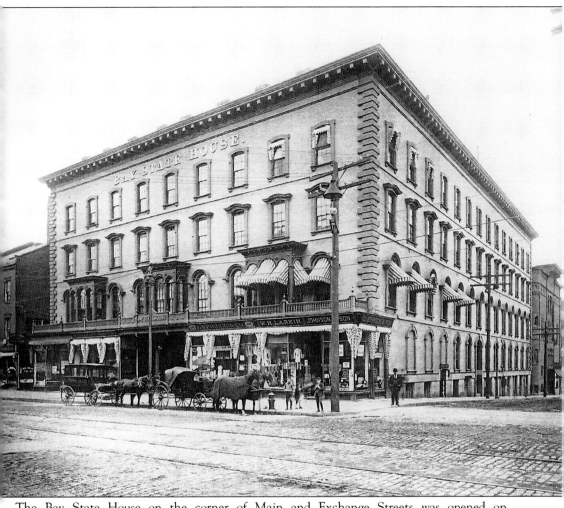

The Bay State House on the corner of Main and Exchange Streets was opened on February 8, 1856, and cost $100,000. The hotel offered such modern conveniences as a passenger elevator, steam heat, and a ladies' and gentlemen's restaurant. It eventually became a landmark, and the political gatherings, conventions, and banquets that occurred within its walls brought many distinguished orators and statesmen to Worcester.

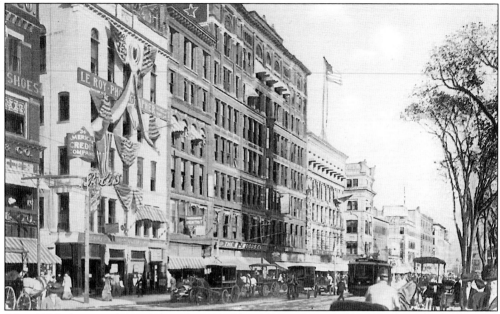

This 1914 photograph is of the Chase Building, located at 44 Front Street. The building is draped with flags, signifying a celebration. LeRoy Photographer, the Poli, and the American Credit Company all occupied the building at this time.

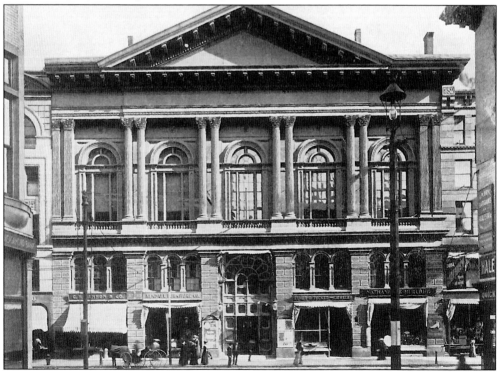

Mechanics Hall was built in 1854 on the site of the Waldo Mansion. Among the many great men who have spoken here are Charles Dickens, Presidents McKinley, Roosevelt, Taft, and Wilson, and Vice President Stevenson, to name a few.

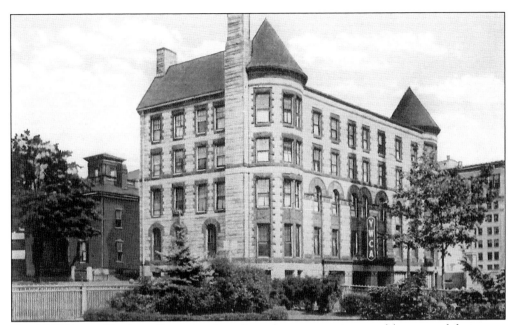

The YWCA on Chatham Street is a boarding place, gymnasium, and home, and features a curriculum of daily activities that focus on improving young women. The principal benefactor was E.A. Goodnow.

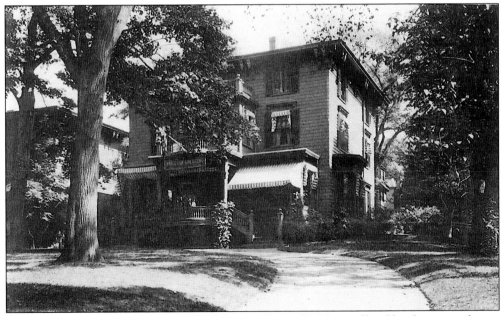

A photograph of the Worcester Girls Club. Mrs. Emma D. Harris offered her home as a house for girls to the Worcester branch of the National Civic Federation on December 1, 1915. The club still exists today, though in a newer residence on 67 Lincoln Street.

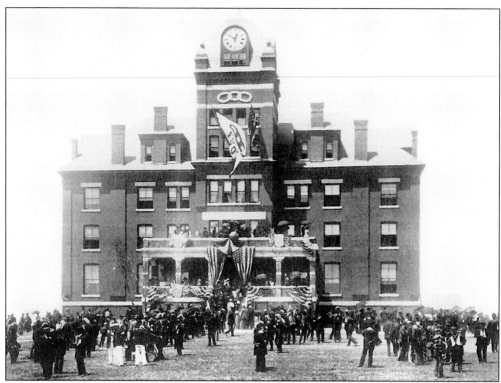

The dedication of the Odd Fellows' Home of the State, erected by the Grand Lodge on Randolph Road in 1903. The new building was as large as the original, and had accommodations for 110 people.

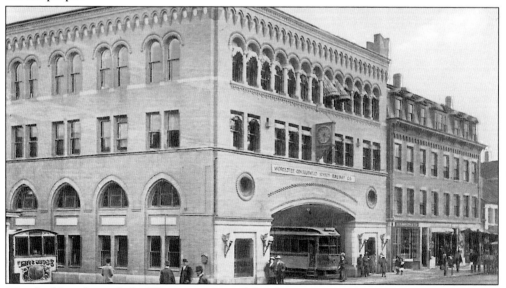

This building housed the Worcester Consolidated Car Barn offices upstairs, and was the entrance to the car barn itself. There were many trolleys kept in the "backyard," and repair work was done on the premises. The WCCB was a conglomerate which operated in every town in the Worcester area, and it leased many trolley lines while buying up others. The Worcester cars had a distinct slim look with a wide railroad roof.

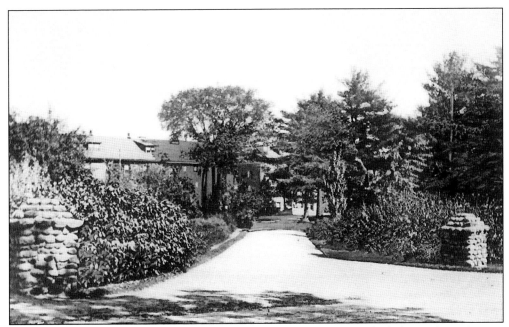

The Home Farm, located on Lincoln Street, was a model institution, both from a farmer's view and as an almshouse. It had its own bakery, cannery, dairy farm, and heating and electrical plant. For many years, a vast number of hogs were raised there as a means of disposing of the garbage collected by the city.

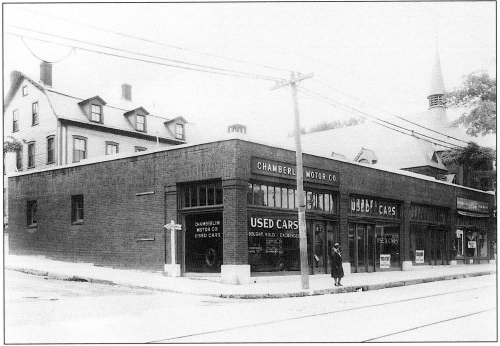

At the corner of Benefit and Main Streets was the Chamberlin Motor Co., which dealt in used cars. The used car business was apparently not very profitable at this point—the building is for rent.

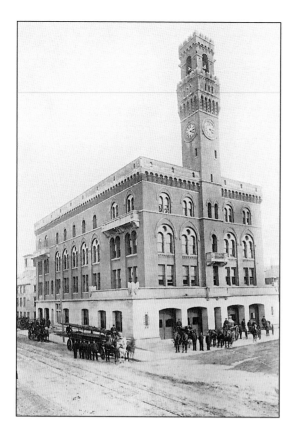

The Worcester Fire Department headquarters on Mercantile Street at the corner of Foster Street. The fire alarm bells were also used as other signals: that school had been cancelled: the police signal was 444-444, while the no school signal was two sets of 3-3-3.

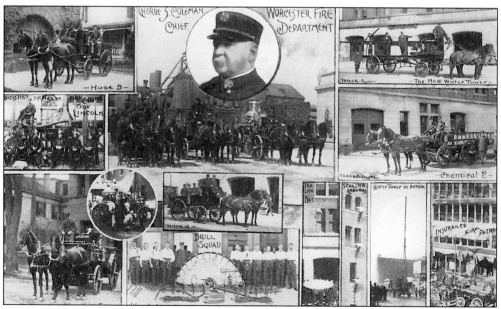

George S. Coleman was the Worcester Fire Department chief engineer from 1903 to 1912. The department was established on February 26, 1835, and is still extinguishing fires and saving lives.

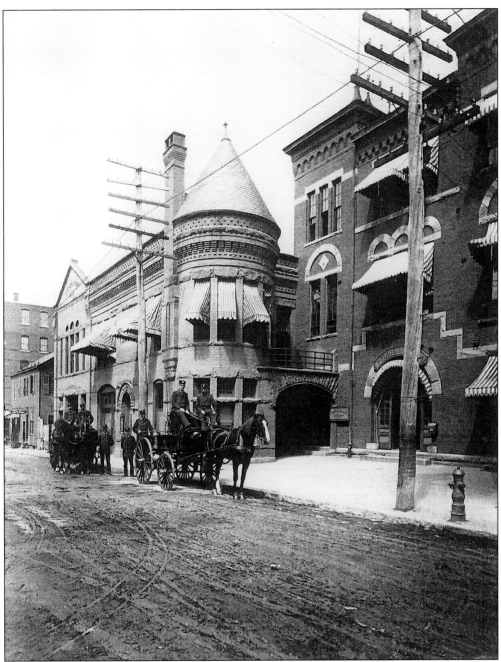

The Worcester Police Station on Waldo street in 1894. The period from 1880 to 1890 was an era of progress for the police department. In 1882, City Marshall James M. Drennan purchased a wagon for the transportation of prisoners, which meant that the custom of dragging prisoners through the streets for a mile or more came to an end. Shortly after this a patrol wagon was bought, and in 1885 the station on Waldo Street was built. In 1887 a police signal and telephone system were installed and by the end of the decade a women's prison had been established and the Civil Service Law had been accepted by the city, making the police force permanent.

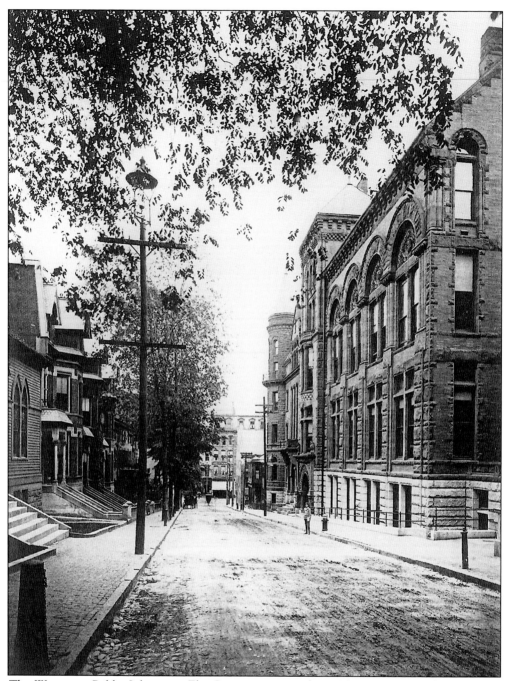

The Worcester Public Library on Elm Street was erected in 1861. Two private libraries, the Worcester Lyceum (1829) and the Young Men's Library Association (1852), united in 1856 and gave their joint collections to the city in 1859, which were used to form the nucleus of the free public library. On December 27, 1859, Dr. John Green gave his private collection of over seven thousand volumes to the city, and left an additional $30,000 in his will toward the establishment and maintenance of a reference section in the Worcester Public Library.

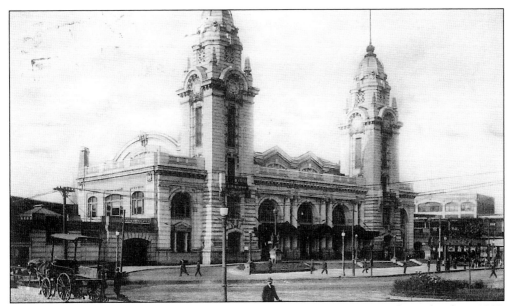

The new Union Station was built in the highly fashionable Beaux-Arts Classical style in 1909 at a cost of over $1,000,000. At one time there were two hundred passenger trains running in and out of the station daily, including trains to New York City and the West Coast.

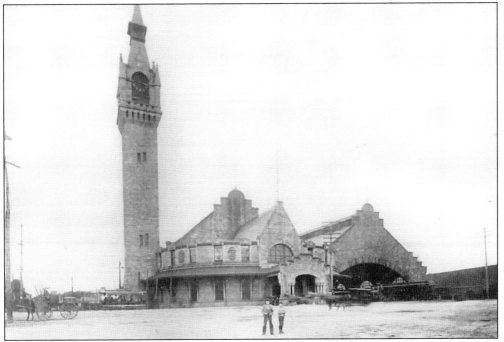

Opposite the new Union Station was the old Union Station, built in 1875 and designed to connect the various railroads entering the city. It was opened by the Boston & Albany Railroad Company on June 1, 1887, but was not widely used until the following summer. At a cost of $800,000, it was the finest building in the city at that time, and was one of the most spacious and artistic stations in the country. The viaduct was built in 1876 to connect the northern and southern roads.

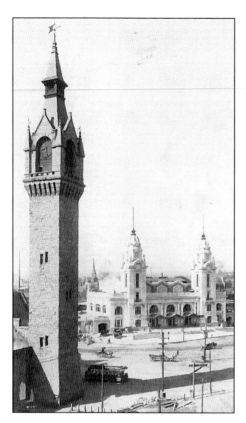

This picture shows the locations of the two stations in Washington Square. The single tower of the old station stood until 1959, when it was torn down. The twin towers of the new station were torn down earlier, in 1926.

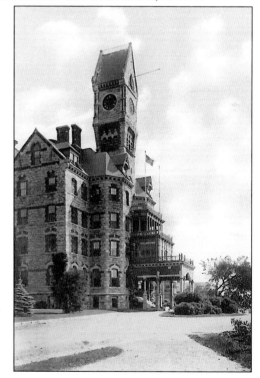

The Worcester Insane Hospital, located on Belmont Street, is the successor of the Summer Street hospital. Built in 1830, the older hospital was one of the pioneer institutions in the country in the treatment of mental diseases and the care of the insane.

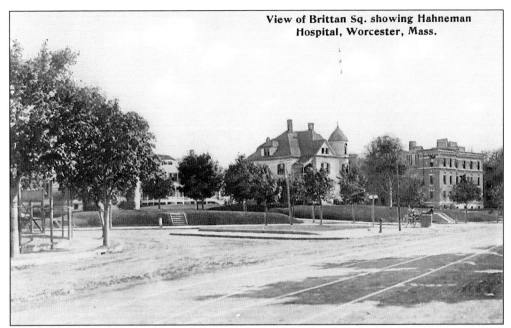

View of Brittan Sq. showing Hahneman Hospital, Worcester, Mass.

Hahnemann Hospital is in the background of this 1915 photograph of Britton Square. On the far left is where Nordgren's Funeral Home is currently located, and a war memorial now stands in the center of the square.

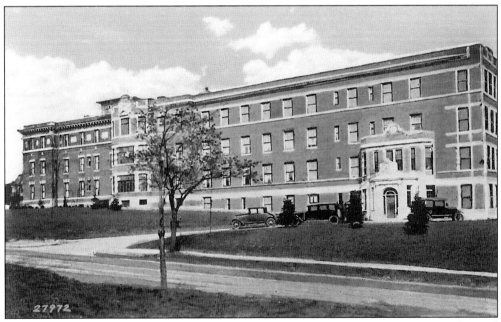

Incorporated in 1896, Hahnemann Hospital began in a house at 46 Providence Street, donated by Mrs. Elizabeth Colburn. The hospital also owes a great debt to David Hale Fanning of Worcester, who in 1907 donated the Roche estate with 2 1/2 acres of land on Lincoln Street and Britton Square.

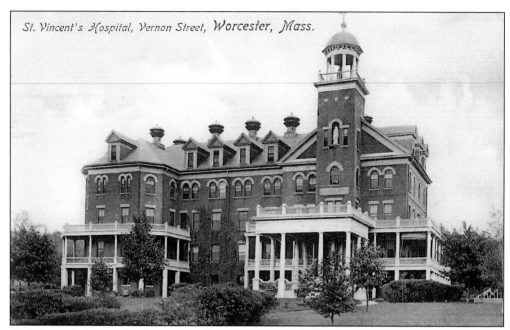

St. Vincent's Hospital, Vernon Street, Worcester, Mass.

St. Vincent's Hospital is located at the intersection of Winthrop, Providence, Vernon, and Spurr Streets. The Sisters of Providence ran the hospital but did not restrict it to Catholics. The hospital opened in 1893 and had accommodations for one hundred people. Expenses were paid with monies collected for treatment, along with gifts from individuals and churches. All of the sisters were graduate nurses. Today, the hospital is run by the Fallon Clinic.

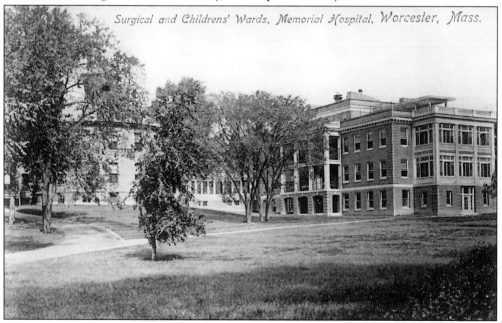

Surgical and Childrens' Wards, Memorial Hospital, Worcester, Mass.

Memorial Hospital was founded by Ichabod Washburn. Washburn died in 1868, leaving a bequest of 750 shares of stock in his manufacturing company toward the creation of a hospital and free dispensary. The hospital began at its present location, in the mansion of Samuel Davis on Belmont Street, with nineteen beds.

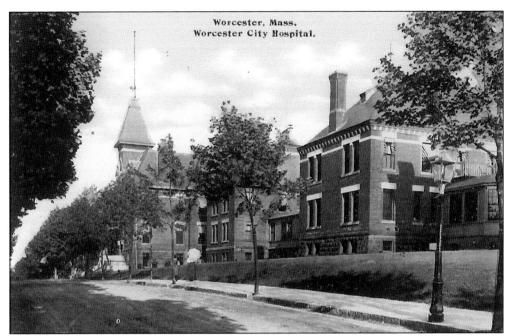

Worcester, Mass.
Worcester City Hospital.

City Hospital, Worcester's largest hospital, was established by an act of legislature on May 23, 1871, and admitted its first patient on October 26 of the same year. It began with only a dozen beds provided in the Bigelow Mansion.

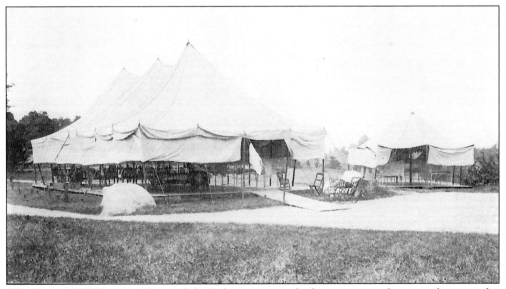

The Green Hill Summer Hospital for Infants consisted of two tents and was used to care for sick children from congested areas of the city. The elevation of Green Hill created healthy, hygienic conditions, which were not always found elsewhere.

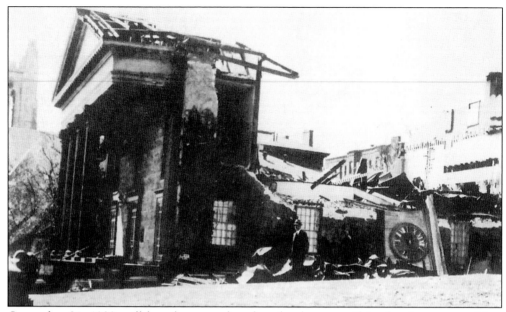

September 21, 1938, will long be remembered as the date a terrifying hurricane swept New England—something never before known to this part of the country. The loss of lives was appalling; property damage mounted to hundreds of millions of dollars and the homeless were counted in hundreds of thousands. The following three pictures demonstrate the extent of some of the damage: here, the Unitarian Church is in ruins, with the tower clock resting on the side of the building.

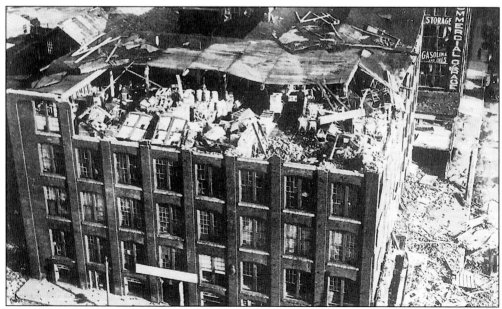

Kane's Furniture store is shown here in shambles. The building is surrounded by debris tossed about by the powerful winds.

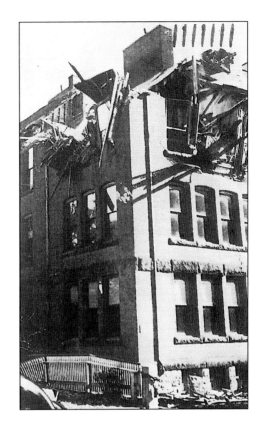

The roof of Classical High School is shown here in ruins.

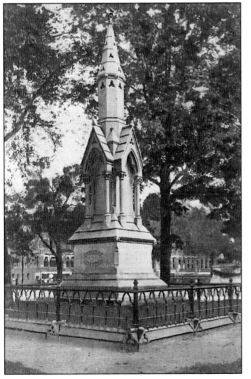

This monument on the common honors Colonel Timothy Bigelow, a patriot and distinguished soldier of the American Revolution. Troops under his command exhibited an extremely high degree of discipline. This memorial was erected by his great-grandson in 1861, and nearby an oak tree was planted honoring his memory.

115

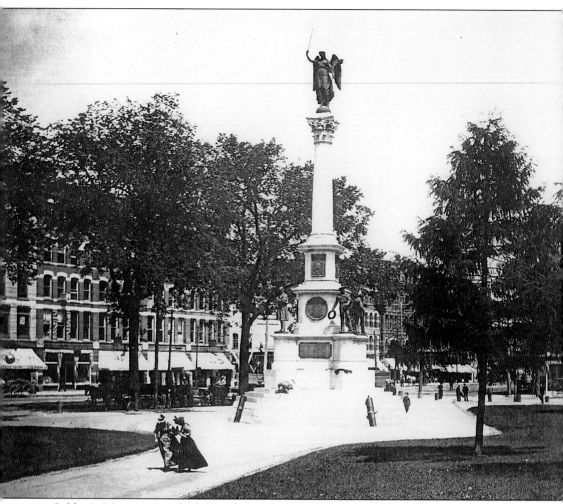

Soldier's Monument, which stands on the northeast corner of the common, is a 65-foot monument honoring the soldiers of the Civil War. The four bronze statues at each corner represent the infantry, artillery, cavalry, and navy units. The inverted cannons at the base of the monument were captured from the Confederates.

Six

Businesses

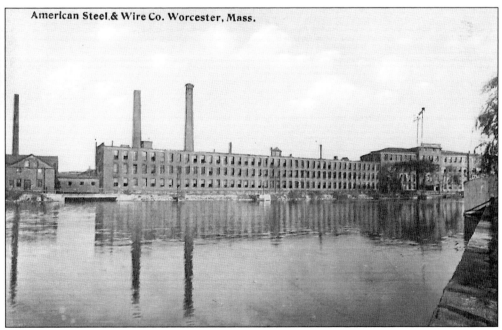

American Steel.& Wire Co. Worcester, Mass.

The immense American Steel & Wire Company was founded in 1831 by Ichabod Washburn and Benjamin Goddard. The business was originally located at Northville, where they made card wire and wire for screens, but in 1835 it was moved to Grove Street. On March 11, 1899, during the period of general consolidation of iron and steel industries, the plant and business was bought by the American Steel & Wire Company.

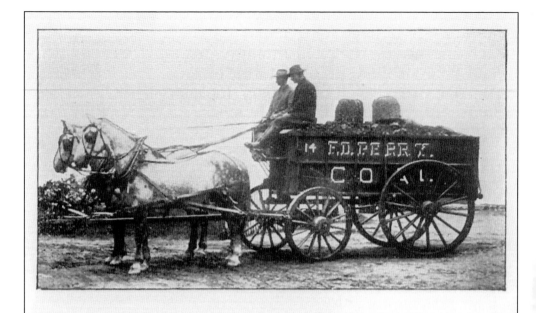

FRANK D. PERRY,

DEALER IN

COAL AND WOOD,

Also Contractor for Stone and Earthwork,

STREET SPRINKLING, FURNITURE MOVING, ETC.

STREET BUILDING AND GRADING A SPECIALTY.

No. 851 Millbury Street.

TELEPHONE CONNECTION.

Frank D. Perry, a dealer in coal and wood, *c.* 1895. From reading the advertisement, it appears that Mr. Perry had many talents.

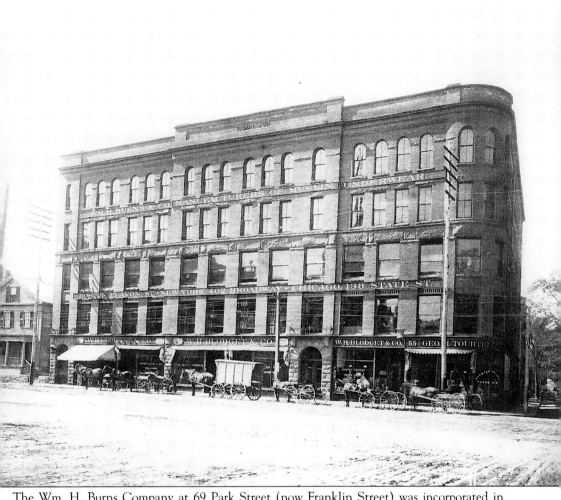

The Wm. H. Burns Company at 69 Park Street (now Franklin Street) was incorporated in 1892 and manufactured ladies underwear.

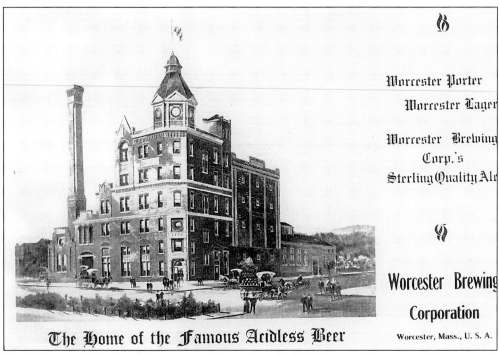

The Worcester Brewing Company was located at 75 E. Worcester Street, on the corner of Henry Street. They were brewers of fine ales, porter, and lager beer. As advertised, they were the creators of the famous "acidless" beer.

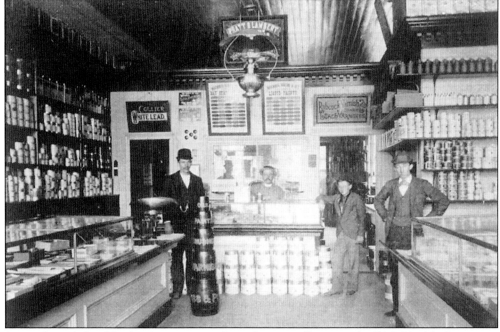

Located at 40 Southbridge Street, across from the post office, was the F.M. Health Company. Inside one would find a stock of paints, oils, varnishes, and other such materials. They also carried machine, spindle, cylinder, dynamo, and Eureka lubrication oils.

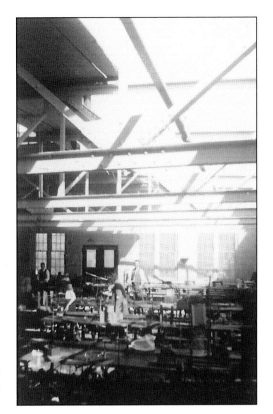

This September 21, 1938, photograph is of Fitzwel Girdles, the day after the devastating hurricane. Note the sun shining through the area where the roof should have been.

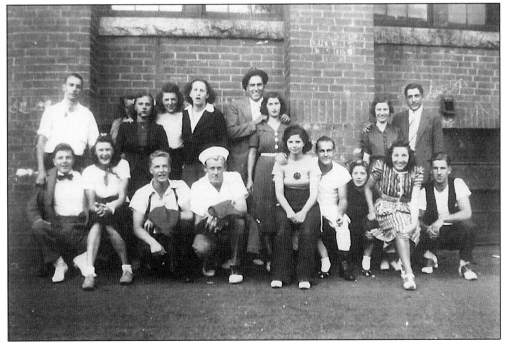

Fitzwel Girdle employees taking a break to pose for a picture in the 1930s.

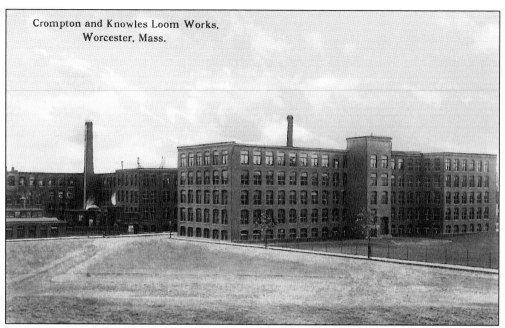

Crompton and Knowles Loom Works,
Worcester, Mass.

The Crompton and Knowles Loom Works were at one time the largest manufacturers of looms in the world. Looms were made by this firm for the manufacture of worsteds, woolens, carpets, rugs, plush, duck, ginghams, silk, sheeting, print cloth, and every type of textile fabric. The business was formed in 1897, when the companies founded by George Crompton (in 1851) and Lucius J. and F.B. Knowles (in 1856) were consolidated.

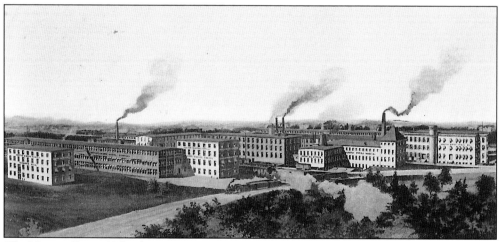

The Norton Emery Wheel Company was one of the most prosperous businesses in Worcester. Purchased by Mr. Higgins and Mr. Alden in 1885, it eventually became the world's largest manufacturer of abrasive products.

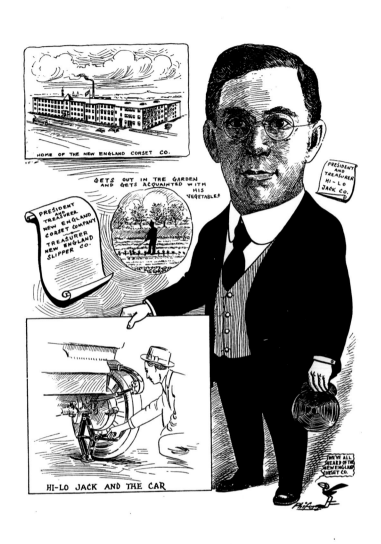

HOME OF THE NEW ENGLAND CORSET CO.

GETS OUT IN THE GARDEN
AND GETS ACQUAINTED WITH HIS
VEGETABLES

PRESIDENT AND TREASURER NEW ENGLAND CORSET COMPANY TREASURER NEW ENGLAND SLIPPER CO.

PRESIDENT AND TREASURER HI-LO JACK CO.

HI-LO JACK AND THE CAR

WE'VE ALL HEARD OF THE NEW ENGLAND CORSET CO.

J. HOWARD JOYNES

208

J. Howard Joynes (see page 35) purchased the New England Corset Company in 1909. He believed in modern methods, not only in reference to office work and machines, but also in terms of providing for the health, comfort, and welfare of his employees. Every employee was protected by a life insurance policy, varying in value from $500 to $1,000, and he abolished the practice of charging workers for the thread they used. On stormy days, the company even provided hot coffee and lunches for its employees. Mr. Joynes was also the president of the Hi-Lo Jack Company.

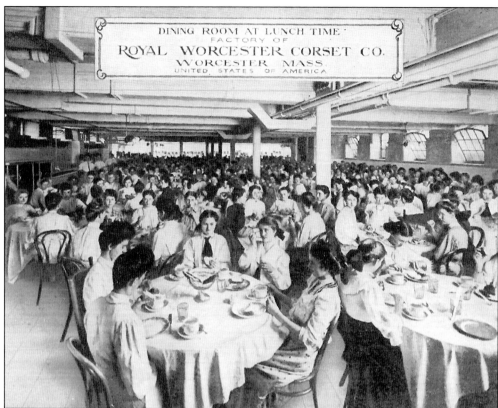

The Royal Worcester Corset Company dining room. The employees were provided with a spacious dining room, adjoined by a reading room featuring leading magazines and papers for employee use only. The heating and ventilating systems were very modern, and the lighting, drainage, and sanitary arrangements were excellent.

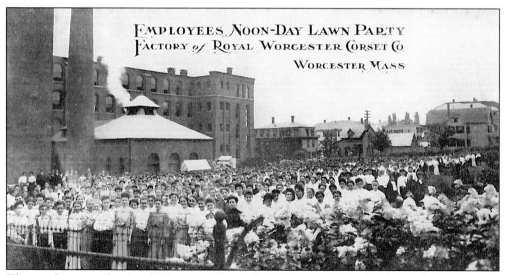

The employees at the Royal Worcester Corset Company enjoying a lunchtime lawn party.

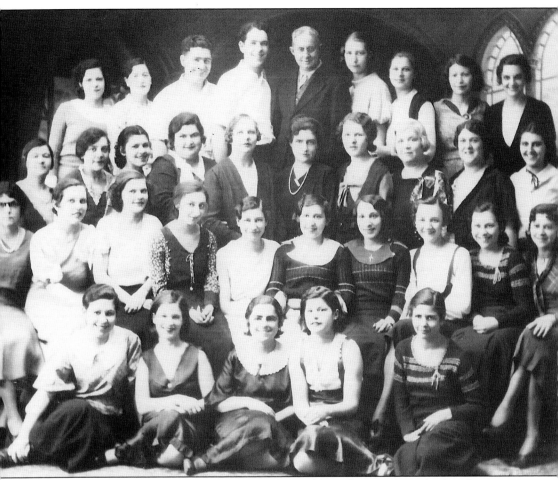

This *c.* 1930s photograph features the stitchers and assemblers of garters from the first floor at Lations.

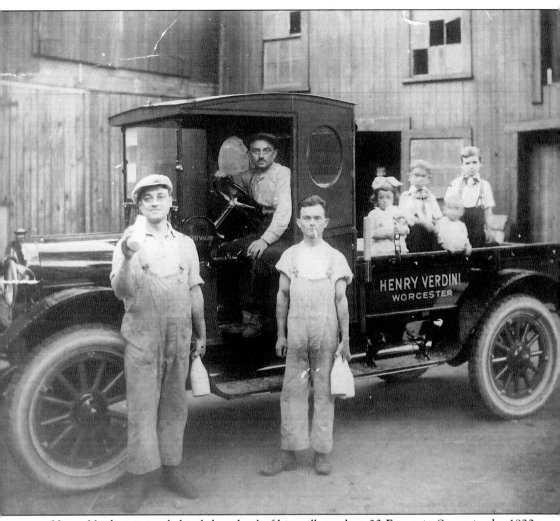

Henry Verdini sitting behind the wheel of his milk truck at 23 Fountain Street in the 1920s. His two brothers Guerino and Gino (the man with the cigarette) are in the foreground. In the back of the truck are his four children: Eva, Carroll, Reno, and Arthur. (Donna Murphy)

Mary Ruggieri and her friend pose for the camera in front of the chicken slaughterhouse on Green Street in the 1930s.

An advertisement for Franklin Cafe Lunch Wagons, based at 22 Cutler Street. Built by J.J. Hennigan, these wagons could usually be found in Lincoln, Washington, Salem, and Vernon Squares. Such wagons were very popular at the turn of the century.

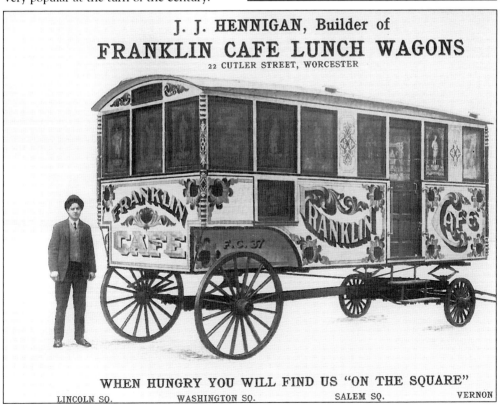

J. J. HENNIGAN, Builder of
FRANKLIN CAFE LUNCH WAGONS
22 CUTLER STREET, WORCESTER

WHEN HUNGRY YOU WILL FIND US "ON THE SQUARE"

LINCOLN SQ.   WASHINGTON SQ.   SALEM SQ.   VERNON

Select Bibliography

Adams, Herbert L. *Worcester Light Infantry*. Worcester, 1924.
Art Work of Worcester. Chicago: W.H. Parish Publishing Co., 1894.
Central Labor Union and Building Trades Council. New York: Boyd Press, 1899.
Forty Immortals of Worcester and its County. Worcester Bank & Trust Co., Boston: Walton Advertising and Printing Co., 1922.
Historical Events of Worcester. Worcester Bank & Trust Co., Boston: Walton Advertising and Printing Co., 1922.
Lincoln, William *History of Worcester*. Worcester: Charles Hersey, 1862.
Nutt, Charles *History of Worcester and its People*. New York: Lewis Historical Publishing Company, 1919.
O'Flynn, Thomas F. *The Story of Worcester, Massachusetts*. Boston: Little, Brown & Company, 1910.
Phifer, L.C. *Men of Worcester in Caricature*. Worcester: L.C. Phifer,, 1917.
Roe, Alfred S. *Worcester in the Spanish War*. Worcester: 1905.
Sawyer, Herbert M. *History of the Department of Police Services*. Worcester: F.S. Blanchard and Co., 1900.
Some Historic Houses of Worcester. Worcester Bank & Trust Co., Boston: Walton Advertising and Printing Co., 1919.
Souvenir Views of Worcester. Maine: L.H. Nelson Co., 1904
Spears, John P. *Old Landmarks and Historic Spots of Worcester, Massachusetts*. Worcester: Commonwealth Press, 1931.
Sutherland, J.H. *The City of Worcester and Vicinity and their Resources*. Worcester: Worcester Spy, 1901.
Wall, C.A. *Reminiscences of Worcester*. Worcester: Tyler and Seagram, 1877.
Worcester and its Points of Interest. New York: Mercantile Illustrating Co., 1895.
Worcester Old Home Carnival. Worcester: Blanchard Press, 1907.